LIVING NIGHTMARES OF ABUSE

Phyllis Benton

PublishAmerica
Baltimore

First printing

ISBN: 1-4137-9156-5
PUBLISHED BY PUBLISHAMERICA, LLLP
www.publishamerica.com
Baltimore

Printed in the United States of America

This book is dedicated to all abuse victims.

May you find an angel.

ACKNOWLEDGMENTS

David Benton, my husband, for being who he is. He is an angel with his tolerance, encouragement and patience.

O. C. Stonestreet III, my mentor, whose guidance, inspiration and friendship have been greatly appreciated.

My brother, David Farley, whom I love, and who has always been there for me.

Chapter 1

Beginning My Life

Mom was sixteen when she married my dad. Dad was several years older than she. She was small, had auburn brown hair and blue eyes, and was five feet tall. She had her first child the year after they were married in 1949—my brother Floyd Robert. We called him Bobby.

Mom, Dad and brother Bobby.

My parents lived in a small house in McKinley, Maine—the town has since been renamed Bass Harbor. My dad bought his first house shortly thereafter, the house my brothers and sisters and I would live in. He paid five hundred dollars for the two-room house. It had no luxuries: no electricity and no running water. Dad built two additional bedrooms on the house shortly after purchasing it.

My sister Jenny was born in 1951, and I was born a year later in October, 1952. Daddy picked out my name. He named me Phyllis after his sister. Everyone called me by my middle name, Diane, though.

I don't remember much before I was three or four years old. I do remember the flowers in Mom's garden very distinctly. She planted lupines, bachelor buttons, sweet William and sweet pea. Mom had fences around her flowers, mostly to keep the animals out but also to keep the kids from picking them as well. I loved the flowers. The colors were so brilliant and they smelled like perfume in the air.

I recall an event, so vivid in my mind, which took place while I was playing outside by myself one day. The State Department was doing some construction work on the road in front of our house. I had been watching them as I was playing. I looked up to see a giant bulldozer coming up our driveway. I ran to our car and climbed on the front bumper and onto the hood. I began screaming and crying. The man driving the dozer saw me, and I could see he was laughing. He then backed out of the driveway and onto the pavement. I don't remember how I got off the car. It was a very frightening experience for me.

A couple of years went by before Mom was pregnant once again with her fourth child, my brother David. From the day he was born he was a mess. His mouth was always wide open and laughing, screaming or just making noise. David was so full of energy. I loved my little brother; he was like a little baby doll to me.

Dad wasn't a tall man but he was kind of stocky, as I recall. His hair and eyes were dark brown, almost black, and he was born with a hair lip. Daddy knew that with another child we had to have more room in the house. He built a set of stairs up to the attic, which would house our new bedrooms. He put a window in each end of the house upstairs so we would have more light and could open the windows to get air.

Bobby, Jenny and I slept upstairs and David slept in the little room below the stairs in a crib.

Brother David.

When my sister Jenny was born she had a bad heart and a bad eye. She had what was called amblyopia, or lazy eye. They said the heart murmur would get better as she got older. She had several surgeries on her eye when she was not much bigger than I was. All of us kids felt terrible that she had to go to the hospital and stay there for several days by herself. We kids couldn't visit her; they didn't allow kids as young as we were to go in. Momma and Daddy got her a Raggedy Ann doll while she was in the hospital. It had striped red-and-white legs and braided yellow hair. My sister absolutely loved the doll. I could hardly wait for my sister to come home from the hospital. I missed her so much. Finally, Momma said, "Jenny is coming home tomorrow." When she returned home my brother Bobby was so delighted to see her he hugged her neck, saying, "I love you." Bobby was always hugging us around the neck. He'd hug me so tight sometimes I could hardly breathe. He seemed to really love us.

It wasn't long before another baby arrived in the family. It was a girl and Momma named her Shari. Daddy really had to make more room now. Even with the new bedrooms upstairs, the house was getting crowded with the tiny kitchen and small living room. He had the floor built for another new room and hoped it wouldn't take long to finish it. I liked sitting on the edge of the new floor outside and watching my dad and some men who were helping him work on the addition.

We always had cats as pets. Momma liked cats. We had one cat named Bootsy because it looked as though it had boots on. Sometimes when I sat outside on the new floor watching my dad work, Bootsy would attach to my dangling feet. He would scare me. I would scream and jump up.

One day Dad started tearing up the boards on the addition and burning them in our wood stove. The addition would not be finished now.

In addition to all the hens, chickens and rabbits we had, we also had a black rooster. The rooster was used for breeding, but he was our pet too. The rooster evidently had a vendetta against Bobby. He would wait for my brother to come out of the house in the morning and then fly up toward his head. The rooster would perch up on Bobby's shoulders and peck his head. The rooster just liked to torment my brother. Bobby would struggle to get the rooster off his neck and then proceed to chase him. He'd be yelling, "I'm gonna get you, rooster!" He caught the rooster a few times and would get his hands around the rooster's neck and commence to shaking him. The rooster would get loose of Bobby's grip and run away. It was like they had a secret game they played together.

Bobby and the rooster.

Soon Momma was pregnant with another child. Momma named her Angela but we called her Angie. The two boys slept upstairs next to the chimney. They each had a single bed. It was warmer on their side than on the side where we girls slept. We'd ask our brothers, "Can we come in your room and put our hands on the chimney before we get in bed?" They would usually let us. Jenny and I slept closest to the stairs in one bed. The two younger sisters slept downstairs at the bottom of the stairs in cribs. Momma and Daddy slept in a small room next to the babies. We had one army blanket per bed but we had flannel sheets to keep us warmer, and also to keep us from itching so bad from the wool blanket.

It got extremely cold in the winter in our little house in Maine, even though Dad got up during the night to put more wood on the fire. It didn't matter how much wood was put on the fire during the night, the air that came through the cracks in the roof cooled the house quickly. Waking up in the morning with ice coating the nails protruding through the roof made it seem that much colder. I was so cold when I'd wake up in the morning that my teeth would be chattering and my whole body shaking. I had to wait my turn to get out of bed. There wasn't room for all of us to stand around at once in front of the wood stove to get warm. Momma got the babies up first to bathe and put dry clothes on them, as they often wet the bed during the night. After each of us would get warm we would hurry to get dressed before we got cold again.

On Saturdays we all got baths. It took a lot of water from the well for everyone's bath. The water had to be heated on the wood stove in a stainless steel tub. The boys were first to bathe. There were only the two of them. Bobby had to help carry the water from the well up to the house for us girls to have our baths. Bobby used to think he was really strong from carrying water up to the house. He got to where he could carry two buckets of water at a time. Bobby would say to me, "Feel my muscles."

I'd put my little hand around his arm. "What muscle?" He'd shake my hand off his arm and walk away.

Dad dug our well with a shovel. He lined the walls and bottom with big rock. It was only about four feet deep but it had a continuous boiling spring; therefore, it never went dry. Dad built a platform over the top of the well so you could stand on top to get water without falling in. There were always eels swimming in the bottom of the well. Dad said that meant the water would always be fresh. I hated the eels; they looked like snakes and I was scared of snakes. Daddy knew I was scared of the eels. Sometimes when he'd go to the well to get water I'd go with him. I liked trying to carry a bucket of water to the house. Dad would grab me and pretend he was going to throw me in the well with the eels. I'd scream, "No, Daddy, stop!" He would laugh and then let me go. I could only carry about a third of a bucket of water to the house. I wasn't as big as a pea.

It was early on a cold, snowy Christmas day. Daddy had been up real early. I had heard him putting wood in the stove and sipping on his hot coffee. I never understood why he wanted his coffee so hot that he had to sip on it in order to drink it. I heard him and Momma talking quietly and some of the kids getting up. We didn't have but only a few gifts under the tree. Most of them were candy bars that were wrapped in newspaper. Christmas was still exciting. Dad was getting ready to go outside. He said while putting on his coat and hat, "Santa came during the night but had to leave the presents outside. He told me he couldn't get down the chimney because he was to fat." Daddy was always joking and making up stories to tell us to make us laugh. Dad went outside.

Bobby said that Dad had just made up a story about Santa. "There's no real Santa Claus. Dad hid the presents outside. Santa didn't really come during the night," he'd say. We didn't know if Bobby was right or not so we ran to the window in the living room, the one facing the outhouse, to see if his footprints were the only tracks visible. The only footprints we saw were one set that Dad had made going to the outhouse and was now making in the glistening, new-fallen snow as he came toward the house. In his arms he carried a big box. There just had to be a Santa Claus. It seemed to be just like Daddy had said. He opened the door and as we gathered around, jumping up and down with delight, Dad tried to get in the house with the big box.

"Move! Move!" he'd say. "Move out of the way." Dad put the box on the floor in the middle of the living room.

We were still jumping up and down and trying to get to the box, and then Momma yelled, "Move out of the way or you won't get anything." Momma did the giving out like she knew what belonged to whom. Jenny and I both got a doll dressed in a pretty lace dress with a bonnet on its head. We both also got a miniature roll of toilet paper. I don't recall what each one of the other kids received but all seemed happy with what they had gotten. None of the gifts were new, but that didn't make a difference to any of us.

13

My aunt Phyllis always made us something for Christmas. One year I remember she made Jenny and me skirts with shoulder straps. One skirt was plaid and one was a solid light orange. We would take turns wearing each of the skirts, so it seemed like we both had two skirts. I loved the things that Aunt Phyllis made for us. She was a good seamstress.

Aunt Phyllis.

Most all the kids in the neighborhood had a pair of ice skates and nearly all knew how to skate. I used to pretend that I was sick so I could stay home to ice skate in the driveway in the afternoon. Oh, I was better by afternoon. Momma knew that I wasn't really sick, but there were days I just didn't want to go to school. She'd let me stay home once in a while.

Gott's Pond was where most of the kids got together to go skating. We went there after school or on the weekend. I wasn't very old, maybe ten or eleven then. The older kids would build a fire by the side of the pond so that when we got cold we could stand by the fire to get warm. We would get old tires and wood from around the pond to burn on the fire. I always had mittens and scarves to wear that had been given to me for Christmas. They got worn out quite quickly with playing on the ice pond and making snowballs. About the time we got so cold we couldn't feel our hands and feet anymore, it was time to go home. It took a half hour or more to walk home. Getting back to the house where there was heat from the wood stove was more than welcoming.

Besides ice skating in the wintertime, there was sledding. There was a gravel pit across from the gas station where we played. The gas station was next door to our house. It had hills made from piles of sand that were used to sand the roads after it snowed. We had sleds but they often got broken or were just worn out from so much use. Tire tubes were great to slide on. The garage had old tubes and only had to put patches on them and they were good to go. Better yet, cardboard from big boxes—you could fly on cardboard. The cardboard was fast but you couldn't stay on long without sliding off. Several of us could get on the tubes together, but there was nothing to steer with. Sometimes we would end up across the road. It was a good thing that most people didn't drive fast on that road. There was also a stop sign by the entrance of the pit. That helped to slow down any cars coming that way. It was a miracle that we never got run over by a car. I did have a close call one day while sliding on a tube by myself. You can go much faster with less weight, and I was really moving. I was headed toward the road and couldn't stop. I was afraid to jump off the tube before I got to the road so I stayed on. When I finally came to a stop, a car was stopped right in front of me in the road. The man in the car rolled down a window and said, "That's a good way to get run over." I quickly got up and grabbed my tube and got out of the road. I didn't slide so fast after that episode and stayed mainly on the small hills and away from the road.

15

Mom and I took a rocking chair down to my great-grandmother's house one night after dark on a sled. It was cold and snowy with the wind blowing. The wind felt as if it was cutting right through your body. Mom said, "Grandma really wants a rocking chair." I don't know why we took it on the sled. It could have been the only way to get it there. Great-Grandma Laura Carter lived in a small three-room house near the ocean and close to the fish factories. On the dirt road where she lived were other houses that looked similar to hers. The houses were side by side, much like you'd see in a mill town. My great uncle Lawrence lived next door to Grandma with his family. Once we got there I was in no hurry to walk back in the freezing cold, but we had no choice. Grandma Laura always had tea brewing in a pot that she kept on her little wood stove. Mom and I both had a cup of tea before attempting our trip back home. Mom and I hugged Grandma and said, "I love you." We hurried back home with the empty sled, and after getting home I sat in front of the stove for a long time to get warm. After you've gotten chilled to the bone, it's not easy to get warmed up again.

We had to wait for the bus to come and pick us up for school even though we only lived a short distance from the school. I liked to walk to school sometimes, even in the winter when it wasn't freezing cold and the wind wasn't gusting, but that wasn't very often in Maine. Over by the school there was a small bridge with ocean water flowing under it. We would go over there to play under the bridge when the tide was low. We'd jump from rock to rock and try to stay on the rock without falling off or slipping into the water. Most of the rocks were covered with green algae that we called green slime and it was very slippery. We would pull it off the rocks and throw it on each other to look like green monsters. If you squeezed the water out of it, it had a spongy texture.

A wild plum tree grew near the bridge. Only a few of us knew of the tree. The plums were a deep purple and sweet when they were ripe enough to eat. David and I would keep checking day by day to see if the plums were ripe yet. If we were lucky, we'd get them before anyone else did, but most of the time we'd only get a few that were left near the top of the tree. The tree had been cleaned off by others who knew of the tree.

difficult temperment

I didn't like school very much. I was hyperactive and found it very difficult to concentrate and stay focused on anything long. Most of fifth grade I was sick with numerous things, including childhood diseases. I missed a lot of school that year, and as a result had to stay behind a year. Another reason that I didn't like school was the kids would make fun of me because the state gave us food and we wore hand-me-down clothes. I would walk home after school wiping the tears from my eyes from my feelings being hurt.

poverty

I once got a new coat—it was new to me, anyway. It was a beautiful burgundy color. I loved that coat but it was too long in the sleeves. Momma rolled up the end of the sleeves. "Now your coat has cuffs."

One day after school was out for the day, I put on my new coat, ready to get on the bus to go home. I heard something jingle. There in one of the cuffs were two quarters. I didn't know how they could have gotten there. I told one of my friends, "Look what was in my coat cuff." I opened my hand that held the quarters.

She looked surprised. "You found them in your coat?"

I said, "Yeah, I heard something jingle and there they were. What should I do?"

She answered in a whisper, "Just keep them is what I'd do."

I was afraid, thinking that would be stealing, not knowing to whom they belonged. I decided I should tell my teacher. I walked up to my teacher when the other students weren't near her and held out my hand. "Look what I found in my coat cuff."

My teacher didn't look very surprised. "Oh, really?"

I said, "What should I do with the money?"

She smiled. "Why don't you hang onto it until it's time to get on the bus, and if no one claims it, you can keep it." I hoped that no one would claim it. I really wanted the quarters. No one said anything so I got to keep them.

The principal of my school was very tall and slender. I was a tiny thing. During the day I would have to walk down the corridor a lot to go to the bathroom and back to the classroom. Mr. Minton, the principal, was always walking the corridor doing his job. I was shy, so usually when I saw him I didn't say anything. One day when I was

17

hurrying down the corridor I didn't see Mr. Minton as he was coming toward me and I ran right into him. It frightened and embarrassed me and I began to cry. He picked me up and started comforting me, "There, there, little one. It's alright. You're not hurt." Later he became my science teacher as well as my principal. He was my favorite teacher. Mr. Minton was very good with young people.

Diane.

My science class had to bring something in for a show-and-tell project. I had a rabbit at home that looked as if he had a black mustache. He was one of the breeder rabbits Dad used to breed with other rabbits. I had named him Bill after Mr. Minton because he too

18

had a mustache. Dad wasn't too crazy about me taking his rabbit to school but he said as he scratched his head, "You can take him if you come home at dinnertime to get him and bring him straight back when school is out." This would be the best project. I did what Dad said. As soon as the dinner bell rang, I grabbed my coat and ran out the door and out the drive. I had to run most of the way to get home and back to school on time. Bill was a big hit, not only with the students but with my teacher. I said, "I named him Bill because the other teachers call you Bill and you have a mustache just like he does." Mr. Minton seemed very pleased and impressed with me and Bill.

My favorite subject in school was art. My art teacher was great. Mr. Woods would take the class outside and have us draw or paint trees. If he saw something that he thought was exceptionally beautiful, he would point it out and have us draw or paint it. He told me one day while outside drawing, "Diane, you are a good student. You are very creative and artistic." I gleamed with pride. He also said, "Maybe you should think about pursuing a career in the art field some day." That seemed like an impossible dream.

At my school, they always put on a play at Christmastime. Jenny and I both got parts in the play. It was a Spanish play where they break a piñata. My part was to break the piñata that was filled with candy. The night of the play, we put on our costumes and waited for the bus to arrive to take us to school. It was very cold outside that evening. We would go outside for awhile and then run up to the house to get warm for a few minutes, then go back down to the end of the driveway again. We waited and waited, but no bus. "Oh no!" I said. "We must have missed the bus."

"We could walk," Jenny announced. "Maybe it's not too late if we hurry." Even though it was cold, we decided to walk over to the schoolhouse. Maybe we weren't too late, maybe they waited for us. When we arrived at the schoolhouse, the play was just ending. I started crying. I wanted to be in this play so badly. All the candy had already been gathered up, and not even one piece did we get. I was upset for a long time over not getting to be in the play.

My brother Bobby loved to write when he was in school. He had

19

said, "I want to be a writer after I graduate. I could write for a newspaper company or something." Bobby got A's in school. He liked to write short stories. He never got the opportunity to write or work for a newspaper company, although I believe he would have made a good reporter or columnist.

Oh dear, here comes another sister. Her name was Lori. It was really getting crowded now. Room was running out. I wished Daddy could have finished that additional room. Shari was now in a bed upstairs and Jenny and I still had to share a bed. The new baby and Angie slept downstairs in cribs below the stairs. Jenny and I would talk after we were in bed. We would get too loud sometimes. With the babies we had to be quiet. That wasn't that easy to do. Momma would come halfway up the stairs with a hairbrush and lean over the railing to hit us with it. "Ow, that hurts!" I'd holler. Believe me, she would hurt me with that brush. One time wasn't enough to get hit. Here she came again. I was hiding under the blanket this time. Hiding didn't help. "Ow, Momma. That hurts. It's Jenny's fault. I didn't want to talk but she made me," I'd yell. Momma always hit whomever was the easiest to get to; it didn't matter if you weren't the one doing most of the talking or not. I was always on the side she could reach the easiest.

Our last sister was born. Momma named her Heidi after the little girl in the story. The little house was full now—not much room and a lot more commotion. I liked staying at my cousin's house on the weekends when it was possible. Our house always seemed so noisy. My aunt and uncle would let me stay at their house quite often. My one cousin and I were close in age and got along really well. I liked spending nights at friends' houses too. One friend in particular, her mom used to give us perms. Damn, I hated those perms. The rods would hurt my head when she'd put them in so tight and the perm smelled terrible. I felt as if I looked like Little Orphan Annie when she was finished.

As a kid growing up I don't remember ever really getting bored, except when I had the measles, mumps, chicken pox and whatever else that was going around. I was the first of us kids to get any of the childhood diseases. I'd be stuck in the house while all the other kids were in school or off playing. That was boring.

Bobby wanted a BB gun so badly. Mom and Dad saved all the money they could scrape together to get him one for his birthday. He was so proud of his gun. I had the mumps so I had to stay in the house. Bobby was going out in the woods to practice shooting his gun, and some other kids were going to watch. I watched from the upstairs window, wishing I could go too. I saw Shari and David running back toward the house, and behind them were Bobby and Jenny. Shari was screaming and David was jumping all around and screaming, "He shot her, he shot her!" Jenny was holding her eye and crying. Bobby was walking beside her, his arm around her. He looked terrified. I ran downstairs to meet them as they came closer to the house.

"Bobby shot Jenny, Bobby shot her," I was screaming to Momma. Bobby said his glove got caught in the trigger, and while he was trying to get it loose the gun went off, hitting Jenny in the eye. Momma went into a rage.

She said, "Give me that gun!" She took the gun outside and broke it, beating it over the wood pile. Jenny had to go in the hospital and have surgery on her eye again.

We always found things to do, though, even if it was making up our own games or finding our own entertainment. Sometimes in the evening, neighborhood kids would gather at the gas station on the corner next to our house to play tag, hide-and-seek, or skunk bushes. Skunk bushes was our made-up game. We created it. It was much like tag but we made up our own rules. Hide and seek was a favorite. Sometimes I didn't like playing hide-and-seek. The older and braver of the kids would hide out back in one of the old cars. It was dark and scary to go out behind the garage alone. When I got scared and couldn't find anyone, I would just give up and go home.

One night Shari and I couldn't find anything to do. We couldn't get any of the neighbor kids together to play any games so we decided to do something ourselves. Shari was a very pretty girl. I used to think she had the perfect nose. It was just the right size and shape for her face. She had medium-length blond, wavy hair and blue eyes. Shari wasn't much of a tomboy like I was, so we didn't do as much together as David and I did. I thought it would be fun to get a rope, each of us go on opposite sides of the road, lay the rope on the road and wait for a car to come by. I told Shari, "When a car comes by, wait until it is halfway on the rope and then pull up." We tried this several times but we were not successful. Finally, after several tries, I hollered at Shari, "Pull up!" We did it this time. The man in the car slowed down, then stopped and started yelling at us. "Hey, you!" I don't think he ever saw who we were in the dark. We ran for the woods and tried to find our way back home. It took us a long time to get home, even though we weren't far from home. I know we kept going in circles.

"Listen. I hear someone talking. Come on, let's go that way," I said to Shari. We hurriedly walked toward the voices. We came out on the main road next to the house where some neighbor kids had gathered. Needless to say, that was the last time for playing that game. Shari and I went back the next day to the scene and found the rope lying across the road where it had been left the night before. We assumed no harm had been done.

I had spent the night with my best friend, Lisa. It was Sunday morning. Lisa asked me, "What are we going to do today?"

"Don't know," I said.

She had a strange look on her face and then said, "I know, let's run away."

I must have looked at her like she was crazy. "Run away? Why?"

"Well, not really run away, but pretend we are and pretend we are serious."

The plan wasn't to really run away in the true sense. It was such a pretty day in the early summer, more like spring. We were very young, just eleven years old, but we thought we were so grown up. We started walking. There wasn't much traffic on the road, especially because it was Sunday and we were on a back road. We wanted to be on a back road in case someone might see us on the main road. After walking for several hours we were getting tired.

"Want to go back?" I asked Lisa. "I'm getting tired."

"What do you want to do?" she asked.

"I wish I had something to eat and I'm tired too," I answered her. It was late in the afternoon by now. A few cars passed us by, but nobody that we knew. It was now starting to get dark and we still had a long way to go to get back home. I said to myself, *if we ever get back home safe, I will never do this again.* Shortly thereafter a car stopped, and it was someone we knew from church. *Someone was listening to me,* I thought. We were so relieved to get a ride.

"What in the world are you two doing out walking this late and so far from home?" the lady asked us.

"We were out walking and didn't know we had walked so far and it was so late," Lisa told her. We were ashamed for what we had done and knew if our parents found out we would be in big trouble. We were lucky it was someone we knew who stopped to give us a ride. It could very well have been a bad person instead. The nice lady dropped us off at Lisa's house. I still had to get home, but it was dark and I was too scared to walk home all that way by myself.

Lisa's mom was furious at us. "Where have you two been all day?"

Lisa lied, "We were walking and didn't know it was so late."

Lisa's mom had a car so she took me home. My parents weren't upset with me for being gone all day. Mom figured I had been at Lisa's house all day. It wasn't unusual for me or my sisters and brothers to stay gone all day. We were free spirits.

Growing up in a small town in Maine, we didn't worry much about things happening like they did in big cities or in today's society. There may have been things going on but we never saw or heard of such things like rapes or murders. It just didn't happen in our small town, and if it did no one knew about it except *the old people.* We called people who were considerably older and wiser than we were *the old people.* It wasn't meant as an insult; it gave them a title to distinguish them from the kids. I spent a lot of time with *the old people.* They were so smart, and they knew a lot of things to teach me. My sisters and I used to go visit Flora Reed. She was one of *the old people.* We would pull weeds for her in her flower garden sometimes to make money. We would earn as much as 25 or 50 cents and sometimes more if she had other chores for us to do. She would always watch her soap operas in the afternoons religiously, and we would watch them with her during the summer while we were out of school. We hung out at Flora and Ralph's much of the time. Flora showed me a lot of things, like how to crochet and knit, and other handy things for a girl to know. I learned a great deal from Flora. She would make pot holders to sell.

I would walk house to house trying to sell her pot holders for her. Of course, I got paid a small percentage of what was sold.

In the wintertime after a big snowfall, a few of us kids would get out the shovels and hit the road as early as we could to get jobs shoveling snow. Flora would generally have us shovel her driveway. Her driveway wasn't very long. We would hustle to get done so we could get other customers. The Braggs lived across the road from Flora. They had a long driveway. It would take a good portion of the day to shovel their driveway. I would save my money to buy Christmas gifts with if it was before Christmas. The rest of the kids did the same. We didn't make much money, and with seven to buy for plus Mom and Dad, what little money we had didn't go far. A candy bar was the usual gift for everyone.

Much of Maine is surrounded by water, and there are also many lakes and ponds. The waters stay fairly cool from the winter season even through the summer. The lakes are natural and very beautiful. I was always a good swimmer ever since I was knee high to a grasshopper, all the Farley kids were. Starting the day off with a bowl of cornflakes and heading for the lake to swim was a usual day for me during the summer. It would take about half an hour to walk to Echo Lake unless we got lucky and got a ride from someone we knew. We didn't ride with anyone unless it was someone at least one of us knew. In the early morning, the lake was still a bit crisp to swim in and usually a light breeze would be blowing. Spending the day at the lake swimming, walking through the trails, and laying around in the sun created a good appetite. Berries we picked were all we had to eat. There were times, though, when we had previously earned a little money from doing odd jobs for people, that we'd walk up to Echo Vista to buy an ice cream cone. Echo Vista was a take-out restaurant that sold soft-serve ice cream cones and a limited amount of food. We never had enough money to buy food, only an ice cream cone. After swimming all day a cone of ice cream helped to fill that empty spot in our bellies.

In addition to swimming in the lake, we swam in the ocean. Jenny and I would swim in the ocean with sweaters on. I have told a few people about us wearing sweaters while swimming in the ocean and one person made the remark, "I can't imagine such a thing." I admit, it does sound a bit strange. The air was almost always cool and with the ocean breeze it made it feel even cooler. The sweaters warmed us before we got in the water. After dipping in the ocean a few times, we'd get cold. It was time to take off the sweaters and put on something dry if we had anything with us and if not, we'd go home.

Jenny had hair about the same color as Mom but she was built more like the Farley side of the family, stocky like my dad. None of us were very tall. My brother David was the tallest in the family. He had curly blonde hair like Shari but hazel eyes.

Mom's sisters would come to visit us in the summer. Most of them were married or getting married. I remember my aunt Grace and Libby more than the rest of my aunts. My aunt Grace had moved to Massachusetts with her husband and Libby to Connecticut. I don't remember where my other aunts lived then.

My brother David, a neighbor boy, also named David, and I used to make boats from scrap wood that we got from the lumber yard. The lumber yard was stationed right on the ocean bank so the wood was easily gathered. Sometimes the workers at the yard would give us old nails that may have been bent or a bit rusty to build our boats with. We would use a rock as a hammer to build our little boats. Our boats weren't anything fancy but they sailed without tipping over most of the time. We had fun sailing them in the ocean, except when we would lose them because of the big waves from other boats going by or from the tides going out.

I learned the art of making and doing things with not much to work with. I once made a skirt for my little sister, Lori. I got the material from some old rags my dad kept for cleaning things around the house. I designed it myself and sewed it by hand with a needle and some old thread. I got the thread from the rags by slowly working it out with the help of a sewing needle. I had seen Mom sew before, mending Dad's and our clothes, so I had some idea how to sew. When I had finished the skirt, I put it on my sister. I was proud of what I had made and wanted to show it off. I took Lori over to a neighbor's house. No one made any comments at all about the skirt.

Chapter 2

Eight is plenty

On Sunday mornings we had warmed-over biscuits and baked beans for breakfast. Momma always made homemade biscuits and baked beans on Saturdays for supper. The night before, she would pick over and wash the dry red kidney beans and then put them in a big white kettle to soak overnight. The next morning they would be puffed up and ready to bake. Mom put a big piece of salt pork and molasses in, and Dad always wanted an onion put in with the beans. The beans were put in the wood stove oven to bake during the day. You could smell the sweet aroma of the beans throughout the house, and getting stronger each time you'd re-enter the house. Dad would cut the biscuits in half, put them on a baking sheet, sprinkle the biscuits with a few drops of water and put them in the oven. The water on the biscuits helped to keep them from getting so crispy, Dad said. Baked beans were always better warmed up again. I always loved the homemade beans and biscuits.

After breakfast we waited for the sound of the horn to blow from Flora and Ralph's car. They'd come to take us to Sunday school. Usually I would stay for church unless I could get a ride back home. If I stayed I would help by walking the babies of some of the adults while they attended church. My grandfather, my dad's dad, would have a fit if he found out that any of us had missed going to Sunday school. He would be over at the house as soon as church was out, go up to Dad and ask, "Why weren't those kids in Sunday school today?" They would talk for awhile and Grampy would leave. Even though he stopped going to church himself, he would tell Dad that was no reason for any of the kids not to go. He would always find out from someone if we were there. Neither one of my parents went to church. Momma had too much to do taking care of all of us with cleaning, washing clothes, and cooking. Daddy had to tend the garden and butcher the rabbits and hens so we would have something to eat.

Some Sundays after Sunday school was over, Dad would take those of us who wanted to go up to my grandfather's house. My grandmother Farley died when I was only three. My aunt Phyllis lived there with Grampy. We would have to wait until she got home from church to see her. Ivan, her son, also lived there with Grampy. Ivan was older than any of us by a couple of years. Aunt Phyllis took care of Ivan after his real mother, Hilda, died of leukemia just a few months after he was born. Ivan's dad left soon after Hilda died and was never heard from again. Hilda was my aunt, and my dad and Phyllis's sister.

Brother Bobby and cousin Ivan.

27

Grampy had an apple tree that was always loaded with yellow delicious apples in season. We picked apples to take home so Mom could make pies and applesauce. In the wintertime, when we would visit at Grampy's, my dad and grandfather would go rabbit hunting in the woods behind the house. They usually came back with a few. Dad would skin the rabbits out behind the old barn before taking them home. Curious as I was, I would watch and ask a million questions. My grandfather died when I was just twelve years old. It was the first funeral that I had ever been to. It was hard for me to understand that Grampy was gone.

Grandparents Evelyn & Merle Farley.

Daddy's mother's maiden name was Lunt. My aunt told me that the Lunt name is Scandinavian, from Demark. She said Henry Lunt came to Newbury, Massachusetts, in 1634 or '35, one of the originals. He sailed from England on the ship *Mary and John*. The Lunts were sea captains, and settled in the northern part of New England, she said. POVERTY

The state (welfare) did help us by giving us food. We'd get American cheese, dried milk, oatmeal and other good things. Our family got a turkey from the state at Thanksgiving and at Christmas a turkey or a ham. The dried milk wasn't much to brag about but it was better than nothing at all. When we ran out of dried milk Momma would say, "Put some water on 'em." I ate many a bowl of cornflakes with water on them. Our family got a lot of things from the state. Back when I was growing up you had food delivered to your house. I didn't mind getting things from the state; it was good to have food and clothes to wear. Some people who knew that we needed the help brought things to the house for us. My older sister always picked through everything before I did. She would take what she wanted and I would get what was left. She did give me a see-through blouse. It was light blue and so beautiful. I couldn't wait to wear it so I put it on immediately. Momma saw me with the blouse on. "Take that blouse off and put some clothes on!" I was heartbroken. Momma broke down later on that day: "You can wear that blouse but put another shirt under it." At least I did get to wear it.

Mom and Dad usually drank hot tea. Daddy liked his coffee, too, but didn't drink it all the time. He had a small jar of instant coffee always sitting on the kitchen table for when he would decide to have a cup. Momma would make molasses doughnuts once in awhile, when we had extra flour and molasses. Mom also made squash doughnuts. She got the squash from our garden. When she was planning to make squash doughnuts she would tell whichever of us kids were handy, "Go to the garden and pick some squash." We would have a good idea she was going to make some doughnuts. Momma would melt lard in a kettle on top of the wood cook stove. She always seemed to know when the lard was at the right temperature to fry the doughnuts. You could smell the magnificent aroma of the doughnuts frying. The smell made me so hungry; I could hardly wait to sink my teeth in one of her hot, sweet doughnuts.

Daddy would have a cup of coffee to dunk the doughnuts in. I would ask, "Daddy, can I have a sip of your coffee?"

Dad would pick up the spoon and hand it to me. "Don't spill it, keep the spoon still." I was careful not to spill a drop. What really made the coffee taste so good was the sweet grease that would be floating on top from the doughnuts.

Daddy worked mostly at the fish factories in towns nearby. In the wintertime the factories would be slow for work. Even when the work was slow at the factories they would try to find something for him to do to keep him working steady. Some evenings in the summer my brother David and I would take a sandwich to my dad at the factory for his lunch. We knew where there were several big thickets of blackberries on the way down to the factory. The berries looked like grapes hanging from vines; they were so big and black. We'd pick the blackberries and hold them in our hands, eating them on the way while walking to the factory. Our hands were stained with purple by the time we got to the factory. Dad couldn't always take something for lunch with him to work. We didn't always have something at the house. When he had money he would give it to Momma to send one of us to the store to get some potted meat and bread if we needed it. Dad ate a lot of potted meat and Miracle Whip sandwiches. I liked potted meat with mayonnaise. I hated Miracle Whip but mayonnaise was too expensive for us to buy.

In the summer, David and I, and sometimes Jenny, would go down to the factory and fish off the wharf. The fishing boats would come in to dock while unloading their catch of fish that day. The boats hitting the waves coming in to dock would spray our half-dressed young bodies with the saltwater. It was cool and we would try to duck the spray and scream as we twirled in circles. When Dad was working he'd sometimes come out to see us on his break to give us some pointers. He would also give Jenny one of his factory hats. She loved to wear them. We only had a line and sinkers to fish with. He'd tell us, "Put out more line, go on the bottom if you're gonna catch flounder." We caught a few flounder but mostly we'd catch mackerel. Flounder was a better fish. It was whiter and had fewer bones than mackerel, but mackerel had a good flavor. Dad would fry the fish in cornmeal and flour in a pan on top of the wood stove.

Dad also worked during the day sometimes, doing odd jobs when he worked nights at the factory to make extra money for food and to pay bills. It was hard to support a big family with limited work available. I remember when he worked for the park service in Bar Harbor. He helped to get the trash at the campgrounds in the summertime. The campgrounds were mostly full with those we called *summer people*. Most of the *summer people* would leave right after Labor Day. Everything then got quiet and slowed down, including work for the native island people. *Summer people* were tourists who came to vacation on the Island of Mount Desert. Daddy would bring home pop bottles that he would find from the trash at the park to take to the store to trade for cash. That source of money would also be gone. He put the bottles that he collected during the summer in the shed to save for when we needed food. He would sometimes give us a few pop bottles to cash in at the garage next door, to buy a bottle of pop or penny candy. We older kids would walk the streets looking for pop bottles to cash in. We would go to people's houses that we knew probably bought pop and ask if they had any bottles they wanted to get rid of. Some people would give us some, but most said they would keep them to cash in themselves. It was hard to find bottles on the side of the road. Most of the kids in our area went looking for bottles.

Dad told me he worked for the Rockefellers in Northeast Harbor, Maine, one summer. He did odd jobs and worked outside in the yard like a caretaker. "They were good people," he said. "They treated me good." It was just a summer job, though, and he had to go back to working a more regular job after the summer.

On Friday nights we'd get to watch TV. The most popular show in our house was a science fiction show called *The Twilight Zone*. It came on at 8:00 p.m. and was only a half-hour show. One Friday night after watching the show I went to bed and had a nightmare about the show. I got so scared that I never watched that show again until many years later. On Saturday nights Dad watched the fights. He would turn the TV on to the fights and tell us, "Either watch the fight or go do something else. I'm watching the fight." That was about the only time Dad watched TV, except maybe to watch the news when he wasn't busy doing something else that needed to be done around the house. I didn't like it when the fighters got hurt or bled. It made me feel funny so I didn't watch the fights.

Our TV was an old black and white set, like most TVs were back then. The old TVs had tubes to make them work. When our TV would go out, Dad would go down to Pearl Jones's house to exchange something to get tubes for the TV. If he had nothing to trade, Pearl would give him the tubes he needed, knowing Dad would square up with him later. Pearl had a nice big white house in Bass Harbor. He had geese and turkeys that ran loose in the yard. When we knew that Dad was going to Pearl's we'd ask to go. We were scared to get out of the car because the geese and turkeys would chase us around the house. One time one of the geese caught me. It was pecking at the back of my legs while I was trying to get away and back to the car. Dad and Pearl did a lot of trading. Dad traded things that he had for money to buy food for us. I remember when Dad took his gun that he used for hunting rabbit and traded it to Pearl. He wouldn't let any of us go with him that day. He seemed sad. He came home with butter and a few other items we needed. I remember Pearl being a good person and I think he and Dad were quite good friends.

Daddy was very musically inclined. They called him lightning-fingered. He was a banjo picker and could also blow a mean harmonica. Dad was adept at just about any stringed instrument. Dad had natural talent and played by ear only. He played with a band later on, in 1964. The band played country and bluegrass music on Saturday nights and for special occasions. The band was named The Country Strummers. He also made several appearances on a local television station to play on *Stacey's Jamboree* on Saturday nights in 1969. Bobby was also very musically inclined and he too had a natural talent and played by ear, but he could also read notes.

On Saturday nights a few of Dad's buddies would come over to the house to play music with him. Dad liked to pick at the guitar, but none of the other guys could play the banjo like Dad, so everyone wanted Dad to play the banjo and blow on the harmonica. The guys

Daddy.

(+) Noalcanol

liked to partake in alcohol but Momma ~~wouldn't allow it in the house.~~
Dad didn't drink. The guys would take short breaks and go outside to
have a little drink, then come back inside to play some more. We
loved for them to play the theme song from *The Beverly Hillbillies*.
"Dad, play Beverly Hillbillies. Dad, Dad, play it," we would all be
yelling. Daddy picked that song really well and the guys would jazz it
up even more as we danced around the kitchen. They usually played
their instruments in the kitchen. Dad would tell the guys, "The
acoustics are better in the kitchen." Daddy wouldn't play the banjo at
all if it was raining outside. He would say, "Sounds awful." Daddy said
the rain changed the acoustics, didn't matter where you were.

As we got older David and I wanted to sleep outside. David and I
were pretty good buddies besides being kin. I was a tomboy anyhow
and hung around the boys more than I did the girls. The girls did such
boring stuff, like putting on make-up or curling their hair, but the

boys always did things that I liked to do. We made tents out of blankets that we hung on the clothesline with clothespins. Dad would give us a drop-cord light to keep outside in case we got scared and wanted to come in during the night. We never did go in. David and I would sleep outside in the backyard on a blanket with another blanket over us. We were very young but we never got scared. I remember waking up just about daybreak and seeing a mink running across the backyard toward the woods. "Look, David! What's that?" I didn't know then for sure what it was until Dad told me, after I had described what it looked like to him. I was very excited to have seen this animal and told everyone that I knew about my sighting.

Other kids in the neighborhood, some of our friends, would come over and we'd make a house out of old chicken fences. We placed the fences on a platform that Dad had started for another hen shed. It was tied together with old pieces of rope and anything that we could find to tie it together with. The younger sisters wanted to sleep outside with all of us. Shari and Angie weren't very old then—"Too young to sleep outside," Dad had said. "They're too little, they'll get scared."

They pleaded with him, "Please, Daddy, we won't get scared."

"Okay, but if you get scared, you won't stay out again," Dad said.

There were about six of us planning to sleep out in the house we had made. The boys really did their very best to scare Angie and Shari by saying, "The coons are coming to get you." Angie and Shari were trying to be brave but they were scared. They wanted to go back in the house. Daddy left the door unlocked because he knew my sisters would probably come back in the house.

I ran to the house to see if the door was unlocked. It was. Angie and Shari were coming. "Run, run!" I was telling them.

"Run!" I heard the boys yelling. "Don't let the coons get you."

We sure were relieved that Dad had left the door unlocked. I generally didn't get scared, but when the boys had Angie and Shari about in tears, I got scared. I knew about the raccoons first hand. When the coons came out in the evening to get in the trash, Dad would hand me a flashlight and say, "C'mon, hold the light so I can see to shoot those damned coons." I knew the raccoons could be out there by the trash.

Dad's car.

Dad had a two-tone green Buick, a 1946 model. He bought it from a man that he knew for a good price. I'm not sure why it quit running, but one day my dad parked it on the side of the driveway. This was a perfect place to sleep at night. "Dad, can we sleep in the Buick?" we'd beg him.

"I really don't want you kids and half the neighborhood in that car."

"Please, Dad, please? It will only be a couple of us. Can we, can we?" we'd beg.

"Go on, you won't shut up til you do," Dad muttered, half-mad because we bugged him so bad.

Momma spoke up, "At least they won't be coming in the house in the middle of the night if it rains, sleeping in the car. I don't want all those kids traipsing in the house in the middle of the night. Ain't got no room for the kids to sleep now. Don't want half the neighbor kids in here too."

PHYLLIS BENTON

Six kids sleeping in the Buick was a bigger problem then we anticipated. We only had one blanket for three kids in the back, and one for the three in the front seat. We couldn't stretch out and the blanket didn't cover all of us very well. We didn't dare go back in the house. That would put an end to sleeping outside at all. We managed to make it until daylight. We knew Dad would be up and we could go inside.

I was tired and wanted to go to bed and get some sleep but knew I couldn't. Momma would be cleaning as soon as she got the little kids washed, dressed, and fed. I lay my head down on the arm of the chair but Momma yelled at me, "If you're tired, you should have stayed inside last night to sleep. Go change your clothes and get a bowl of corn flakes. You're gonna help me hang out clothes."

At Halloween we'd get a group of kids together to go trick-or-treating. Bobby and some of his friends hid in the woods by the graveyard until we would come by. They'd jump out with fur coats on. They looked like gorillas and were making sounds, "Grurrrrr, grurrrrr!" We screamed. Bobby knew we were really scared so he peeked out and whispered, "It's only me. Don't be scared." We pretended that we didn't know they weren't real gorillas and continued to scream while running up the road.

David was mischievous, always cutting up or doing something to make someone mad. I remember one day like it was yesterday: Momma was doing laundry in the kitchen with the old wringer washer. David had been outside and had found a green garden snake. He went in the house while Momma was outside hanging clothes on the line. David placed the snake on the top of the wringer, then ran back outside. Momma came back in the house. She reached for the cover of the washer to get more clothes to wring and hang on the line. Momma saw the snake. She didn't actually scream, but just made a loud squeal. Of course David took off long before she could catch him. I don't remember seeing him around the house for some time. He knew not to come home for a while. Momma would have switched him with a willow branch.

Momma always did the spanking except one time that she insisted Dad needed to do the punishing. Dad didn't like to spank us, and

36

after the one time that he did, he said he would never do that again. On the other hand, Momma had no problem getting a willow and hitting us. She would leave welts on you if you couldn't get away from her in time. I never got switched too many times. I tried not to make her that mad or I would find a way out of something that I did that I wasn't suppose to so I wouldn't get switched.

We had a better use for willow branches. We would tie string to one end of the branch and pull it tight until it was shaped like a bow, then tie the string on the other end. Willow branches are flexible and strong. They were easy to work with. We cut more willow branches and made arrows and put arrowheads on them. We would find a rock that was flat and had a point on it and tie it on one end of the willow branch. Our bows held up well and we only had to replace a rock now and again that would come off the arrow. Bobby would sharpen the end of the willow with a knife for arrows. They worked well too.

Jenny had the job of watching us one day while Momma had to go somewhere. David and I got her so mad tormenting and teasing her that she chased us around the house with a broom. She got madder and madder when she couldn't catch us so she threw the broom at us. We took the broom to play with and wouldn't give it back to her. "Better give me that broom. Momma's gonna switch you when she gets home, if you don't give it to me." When Momma got home, Jenny got in trouble for letting us play with the broom. "They wouldn't give it to me, Momma," she said. We didn't want to tell Momma that we wouldn't give Jenny back the broom; we were afraid she might switch us with the willow. If Momma was busy or it was raining outside and she needed a willow to punish one of us with, she'd tell one of us, "Go outside and get me a willow branch." None of us wanted to get her a willow so we'd go outside for awhile. Even when it was raining, we would be outside most of the time. Mom would forget about the willow branch after awhile.

Strawberries grew in abundance across the road from where we lived. It was hard to find the strawberries in the tall grass. After the grass got so high, the State Department would bring out the big mowers and cut the grass, much like they do today. It made finding the strawberries much easier. The strawberries grew fairly large for wild berries. Sometimes we'd get as many as a quart and could sell them to the local store.

About a week after the grass had been cut, it was dry and light. Behind the house there was a maple tree that we would climb, swing on one of its limbs, and let go and fall to the ground. I don't know whose idea it was to do this but it seemed like a good plan. One by one we'd go across the road and get an armload of hay, then run behind the house and out in the woods. We thought if Dad saw us he might get mad so we tried to avoid him. "Uh oh, Daddy sees us," I told the others. We nonchalantly continued to carry the hay, waiting for Daddy to say something, in hopes that he wouldn't.

"Hey, hey, what are you doing? Don't put that stuff in the woods. That's not our woods. Take it all back across the road." As he was yelling he was chasing us and we were running to avoid being caught. Dad was really upset. I hadn't ever seen him so mad. He yelled at us again, "After you get that back across the road, go upstairs and stay there." He got in our car and left. We brought back most of the hay but left a small pile. Surely that wouldn't hurt anything. We went in the house and our friends went home.

"Daddy said we had to go upstairs and stay there, Momma. He didn't say how long. How long we gotta stay up there, Momma? Dad didn't say."

"You better stay till he gets back. You made him mad for him to leave like he did. Guess he'll be back in a while. He's at Pearl's I guess." Momma sighed like she was tired.

Out in the woods near where we played in the maple tree there was a clearing. There were no trees or bushes that grew inside the clearing, only moss and some grass. It was surrounded by solid rock that looked like a circular bench about 15 feet long and about a foot high. It was our play house. Us girls would take anything that we could find out in our make-believe house, like old dishes, pot and pans and just things that other people had thrown out as trash. Next to our play house were rock ledges. We climbed down the rock and dug in the ground for buried treasures. We found golf tees and old bottles.

We had paths all through the woods that we made from going

through the woods so much to get to the opposite side of the road from where we lived. It was shorter to cut through than to have to walk all the way around the road. The section of woods was in a triangle surrounded by the roads.

Shari, Angie and I would hunt little men in the woods. We had been told by my grandfather, Bert McNaughton, that where the ground had a hump or a hole, the little men lived. Bert was Momma's dad. We would visit him when we went to see our grandmother, Marion. Marion was Momma's mother. Marion and Bert were divorced but both lived in Bar Harbor. Daddy didn't like to take us kids to visit him. He said Bert was nothing but a drunk and didn't want us kids to be around him, but Mom was insistent on seeing him. She would tell Daddy, "He's my father, no matter if you like him or not." I liked Bert. I thought he was funny when he told us stories. He was always drinking from a bottle when we were there.

I really wanted to find one of those men. I believed what my grandfather had said. I would hunt for hours in hopes of finding one. My sisters would give up, saying, "There's no little men that live in the woods. That's just a made-up story." I could picture what the little men must look like. They were only about six inches high and wore green pants and jackets, with pointed hats and boots. I thought if I could just find one, I would keep him and take care of him myself.

I had been told by another relative that the McNaughtons—who were originally from Scotland and had later migrated to Ireland—came to United States in the 1800s on a ship named *McNaughton*, and that they came from a long line of drunken Irish.

We also had a camp not far from the town dump. We would go through the woods to the dump and find things to put in our camp. Dad would sometimes bring things home from the dump too. "People throw away good stuff," Dad would say.

My mom took a lot of pictures of us as we were growing up. She always had the camera out, taking a picture of one of us doing something. The family used to do things together. As a matter of fact, we did things together quite a bit. We used to go down to a place called Ship Harbor; it was down by the ocean. Mom would pack sandwiches and whatever else she could find for us to eat. We always

39

had Kool-Aid to drink. Sometimes we would walk all around the big rocks on the shore for what seemed like miles and miles. Dad had an old, black two-seater coupe at that time. Momma would hold one of the babies on her lap, three kids stood behind the seat in the front and the rest of us piled in the trunk. Cranberries grew plentiful on the ocean banks in the marshy areas. Momma would lay baby Heidi down on the edge of the bank while we picked berries. I would watch Heidi to make sure she didn't roll off the bank and into the water. It frightened me to think of her falling into the water. We would all pick berries for hours. It got boring picking berries after a while and we had picked buckets of them. That was plenty for Mom to make sauce with. We'd go off to play on the big rocks. I liked to hunt for crabs, periwinkles, and pretty rocks. I would move the seaweed quickly on the rocks to uncover the tiny crabs. Mom would holler at us, "Come on. Help get the little kids and carry this stuff." We would grab something and start up the trail, skipping and jumping around. Momma would get on us, "You're gonna spill them berries if you don't watch where you're going." If we continued to act up Daddy would give us a little kick in the butt to remind us.

Wild red raspberries and blueberries also grew in abundance in Maine in the summer. The local stores would buy about any kind of berries they could get. Tourists would buy them as fast as the store could get any. Picking berries was a good job for us and an easy way to make money. We picked blueberries, blackberries and raspberries. Mom would often tell one or a couple of us, "Go pick some raspberries for supper." We'd walk over to Long Hill to pick berries that grew at the top of the hill. The bigger and sweeter berries were the ones that grew entwined in the brush piles. They were harder to get to and we had to climb up on top of the brush. The brush was from trees that had fallen from the wind and fires. When we got home with the berries, Mom would wash them and put them in a bowl and add sugar and evaporated milk. You could smell the biscuits that she'd already have browning in the oven. We couldn't eat until Dad got home from work. The big bowl of raspberries would be gone in no time.

At the store, when their bananas started turning black, they would sell them to Dad for ten cents a pound. He would bring them home and Mom would get started making the biscuits. She would do the same with the bananas as with the berries, adding milk and sugar, except the bananas she would mash first. The bananas, like the berries, would be gone in no time. Sometimes I would still be hungry after supper but everything had been eaten. I remember times of going to bed at night and being so hungry that I couldn't go to sleep.

We'd also go to Wonder Land, one of the parks on the island, to walk and play on the rocks while Mom and Dad relaxed and played with the little kids. Some evenings we would go on a ride to Sea Wall. Dad would park the car and we'd get out and watch the waves in the ocean and run on the ocean's edge. We would chase the sandpipers that ran on the beach but they were too fast to catch. I liked to hunt for treasures that may have been washed up on the sand. I hoped I could find a bottle with a message in it. I had read about people putting messages in bottles and throwing the bottle in the ocean to be found by someone a long ways away. There were always many different types of boats out in the ocean to watch. Sometimes we'd see big ships way out in the water. We decided that they must be pirate ships. Pirate ships came in to Ship Harbor years ago and some of the ships sank, losing all their treasures. When the tide was out we could walk across to the other side. We'd sometimes walk across looking for treasure. I loved the ocean. The ocean was full of adventure.

Chapter 3

The Turning Point of Unhappiness

When I was in the seventh grade, my mom was pregnant again, but this time there were complications. Mom was losing this child. She had to go in the hospital to have surgery. My parents didn't have anyone to care for my younger sisters who weren't yet old enough to be in school. Dad had to continue to work to pay bills and feed the family. I stayed out of school to help out with my sisters until Mom was strong enough to come home and take care of them. Soon I was way behind in my schoolwork and getting very discouraged. I wished I could quit school because I had missed so many days, but I was too young. I had to stay back yet another year. School kept getting harder for me and I hated it more and more.

I had my first baby-sitting job when I was eleven. I took care of a six-month-old boy for a working couple during the summer. Dad told the couple that I was a very responsible young girl and I helped care for my own brothers and sisters. I made enough money baby-sitting that summer to buy some new school clothes and a pair of new sneakers to start school in. We didn't get many new clothes, usually one new outfit each and a new pair of sneakers to start the school year. It was nice to have the money to buy new things with. I decided that I was going to baby-sit every summer from then on so I would have money to buy new clothes like other kids had.

We were growing up. My brother Bobby would be graduating from grade school soon. He being the first one in the family to graduate, it was exciting. Graduation day was here. My big brother, Bobby, was going to graduate. He was so proud of himself and we all were too. When the ceremony was over and Bobby had his diploma, he and some friends from the graduating class came by our house. My brother looked very handsome in his suit with a white carnation pinned on this lapel. That was the first time he had ever worn a suit, to my knowledge. Bobby grinned from ear to ear while waving his diploma in the air. It was hard to see him with all his friends gathered in front of him in the front yard. Bobby wasn't tall, and he was built like Mom, on the small side.

Times were getting difficult at home now. Mom and Dad were starting to argue a lot. The little kids would cry when they would hear them argue. I tried to entertain them in hopes they wouldn't hear the arguing. I didn't know what they were arguing about; it was just a lot of yelling back and forth between them.

Mom started going off some during the day, to get away from things, she said. Then she started inviting men friends over during the day while Dad was at work. One man in particular came over more often than any others did. I'd come home from school and he'd be there at the house. I didn't like him; he wasn't a nice person. His name was Nelson. He would try to touch me where he shouldn't, and it frightened me. He began trying to touch my sisters as well. One day while he was at the house, he became quite insistent on touching me. He put his hand up under my shirt and tried to touch my breast. I was too young to be developed much. I squirmed to get away from him. He pretended that he was playing a game with me but I didn't like the game. "I'm just playing with you. Come on and sit on my lap. I won't hurt you." I ran from him to the stairway but he followed me. I was at the top of the stairway and still he continued to chase me. I knew I had no options as far as getting away from him. I looked at the window and threatened to jump if he wouldn't leave me alone. He laughed at me and continued to come up the stairs toward me. I didn't think about anything else except getting away from this horrible man before I jumped to the ground. I didn't get hurt from the jump but I was terrified. I went around to the front of the house. There he was, outside, waiting for me. I ran toward the wooded area behind the house to get away.

Dad knew that this man came over to the house when he wasn't there. Momma would say he came over to see the kids or to take her somewhere that she needed to go. I didn't dare tell Dad what the man had done to me. I didn't understand what was going on and why Momma allowed him to come over and do this to us. I told Mom what he tried to do to me but I felt that she knew anyway. I told her that he tried to play games with me and tried to touch me in places he shouldn't. She ignored me like I hadn't said anything to her. He still tried to touch me after that day when he could get close enough. I avoided him as much as possible and disappeared from the house when he came over.

One day Mom left us. Dad was left to take care of eight kids by himself. We didn't know where she had gone at first, but then we found out she had left with the man I despised. I felt betrayed. My life was turned upside down, as well as the lives of my siblings. My brother Bobby changed so much after my mom left. The dreams that he once had of being somebody and maybe becoming a writer were gone. Bobby just gave up on everything.

Dad tried to find someone to care for my two youngest sisters. He did find someone to care for them for a few weeks but she said she couldn't continue to care for them with no money to buy food for them. Dad couldn't afford to pay for a sitter or to give any extra money for food to feed them during the day. It was hard enough to feed all of us at suppertime as it was. I stayed home from school for a while to watch them again. Dad didn't know what else to do so he let me. After a few weeks of being out of school we got a visit from social services. It was explained to Dad that I could not miss any more school to care for my sisters. They told my dad that they were looking for foster care for the children.

Heidi and Lori were the first to go. They were to go to a foster home together; they wouldn't be separated. They were both very scared. They would cry over anything. They needed their mother like we all did.

Lori was so tiny. She had light brown hair and hazel eyes. I would talk to her about going to a new home, hoping she wouldn't be so scared. The tears would well up in those big eyes but she would hold

Sisters Heidi, Lori, and Angie Farley.

them back, trying to be brave. Heidi, the youngest sister, stayed close to Lori most of the time. Heidi reminded me of Dad's side of the family more. She looked stockier than Lori. There wasn't much difference in height. Neither one of them understood what was happening, only that they had to go away from their family.

I had a young friend named Ted. We would go over to his parents' house and hang out and listen to music, and sometimes I would stay for supper. Ted had a younger sister. She was a freshman in high school. She helped me to make my first dress. It was pink and white. She was always nice to me. I would lay out on the roof of the building with her in the summer so we could get a tan. I couldn't stay long; it was too hot on that dark roof. His father and mother were both good cooks. Ted's dad would make great spaghetti. Their origin was Italian. I hung out at his house quite a bit. His parents knew of the problems we were having at home with my family and tried to help when they could. My sister Shari would hang out with Ted and me on occasion. She felt lost like a puppy like the rest of us did and needed to be with family. Ted's parents got to know Shari, and with help from Teddy, it was arranged that Shari could stay there.

Sister Shari Farley.

Angie had a friend who lived just up the road from us. She would go up to her friend's house to play several times a week. Cheryl, Angie's friend, wasn't an only child but had been born later in her parents' life, so it was as if she were. Dad and I decided to go talk to

Maxine, Cheryl's mom, to see whether or not she would consider taking Angie in as a foster child. The family agreed to take her in and so did the social worker.

My sister Jenny had already moved in with a friend of hers. She and Emma had been friends for a long time and were the same age. Jenny never stayed home much anyhow. She was over there practically all the time, or somewhere else. Jenny and I didn't hang out much together. She had older friends and she and her friends thought I was too young to hang with them. Emma and her family just lived around the corner from us. David, Bobby and I were still living at home.

David and I thought we would help Dad by cutting down some trees for firewood. We went in the woods beside the house and cut down several white birch trees. An ax and a hand saw is all we had to work with, but that was all Dad ever used. We cut down the birch trees with the ax and sawed the wood up into small logs. We carried the wood to the house, took out the wood that was already in the shed, and replaced it with the new wood. We were excited to see Dad get home. He would be so pleased with us when saw what we had done for him.

Gosh! Dad sure was mad. He started yelling, "Get that wood out of here!" and then he'd yell again, "and put that other wood back in here!" Dad didn't even wait for us to move all the wood back before he started moving it himself. We had not only cut trees from someone else's property but new wood is green and won't burn until it is seasoned for about a year. As young children, we didn't know that. David was so upset with Dad for yelling at us. He said he wanted to live somewhere else too, not with Dad anymore. David has always been headstrong. When he said something, he meant it and it took a lot to change his mind. He meant it in this case. David didn't seem to care, at that time, where he went to live. He was mad at Dad and wasn't going to live at home anymore.

David was sent to a foster home in Bucksport, Maine, with a family that was well-off. They thought the world of him but David was rebellious and gave them a hard time, so he was moved to another home.

David had been helping out at a nearby machine shop after school and on weekends before he had been sent to the foster home in Bucksport. The people who owned the shop said they wanted to teach him how to run the machine shop. They liked David and took him into their home.

I had an old bike that I used to ride. I would ride it everywhere. The brakes were worn out so I had to be careful when I rode it. When I was ready to get off my bike, I had to slow down as much as possible, let go of the handle bars and jump off. One day while I was riding, the leg of my jeans got caught in the chain and I didn't realize it. When I jumped off I fell to the ground and the bike landed on top of me. I was knocked unconscious. When I woke up my head really hurt and I could barely see anything. I could see objects but not distinctly. I was close to my neighbor's house so I staggered the rest of the way there. I told Rebecca, Emma's mom, what had happened and she took me to the local doctor immediately. The doctor said I had a severe concussion and needed to go to the hospital. It took a couple of hours before they could locate Dad. He finally arrived at the doctor's office. Dad and Rebecca took me to the hospital in Bar Harbor, where I stayed for two days. Dad came to see me as soon as he could each day after he got out of work.

I wasn't worried about going into a foster home myself. I had already been cleaning, cooking and doing things around the house that I learned to do from my mom. I already knew how to sew and all the things that Flora had taught me. I thought that would be enough of a reason for them to let me stay with Dad. Being twelve years old is a hard time for a young girl, not quite a woman but still not a kid. Social services only saw it one way.

We had just finished eating supper and I was washing the dishes. Somebody knocked on the door. Dad went to the door and there stood the person who told us that I had to leave my home, my brother and my dad. They had already found a home for me in a town a long ways from home called Calais. The lady from social services said the people I was to stay with had two young children and needed someone to care for them while they both worked on the weekends. The social worker said to me, "You will love the children." My foster

48

father, James, was a manager at a big hotel in town and his wife, Wendy, worked there at the hotel on the weekend as a waitress.

After the woman from Social Services had left, I cried and pleaded with my dad not to let them take me. I told him that I was old enough to care for myself and could take care of him as well. He told me he had no choice in the matter, they could do whatever they wanted. "It's the law," he said. I was too young to be on my own with no proper guidance, the woman told us.

A few days later the social worker returned to take me to my new home. I had just gotten home from school. Dad was still at work. I got my things and put them in her car. She took me to the factory where Dad was working. I went in to say good-bye. I held back the tears as I left my dad. I was scared, missed my family already, and had no idea when I would ever see any of them again.

About a month later, Ted wrote that he and his family were coming down my way to visit their family in a town nearby to where I now lived. He said he would come by to see me at that time. I knew where his relatives lived. I had been there with his family before to visit. It was so good to see familiar faces again. I wished my sister Shari had come with them, but she hadn't. My foster mother Wendy didn't like anyone to come to visit me. She didn't even want me to be in touch with friends that I had known back home. She said it just confused me and made it harder for me to adjust. She said I needed to make new friends. Those visits and letters were the only thing that I had to look forward to anymore.

Wendy tried to act as if she were my sister, listening to my music and dancing around my bedroom with me. I didn't like it. She was such a phony. I didn't need any more sisters; I had five already that I needed to be with, instead of being there. I couldn't hang out with anyone who was from a low-income family or wasn't well-known in the town. I wasn't allowed to go to the shopping center or go anywhere unless I was with my friend, Ann. Ann was a nice girl and from a good family. They weren't wealthy, but middle class. They lived in a medium-sized house, nothing fancy, but nice. Sometimes on a Friday or Saturday evening we would walk across the Canadian border to St. Stephens to watch a movie at the theater. We didn't have a theater in Calais. There was a bowling alley in Calais but we weren't allowed to go inside because they served alcohol. We went to the early show at the theater so I could be back in time to baby-sit for James and Wendy.

This one particular boy at school had a crush on me and I liked him too. When we were together we would talk about our families and things that we both liked. We would talk at school and he would walk part of the way home with Ann and me after school. He also called me at home when I would baby-sit on the weekends. His family was poor and he didn't have much of a family life. His dad no longer lived at home with him and his mom worked a lot. Music was always something that we liked to talk about. We both liked the same type of music: rock and roll. That's when the English groups were popular, like the Rolling Stones and the Beatles. I liked classical music too but wouldn't tell anyone; they would think I was weird.

I would sneak out of the apartment through the window in the baby's bedroom on Saturday morning and meet my friend. I had to get on the roof of the apartment building where we lived and climb down the fire escape to the ground. We would walk to the shopping center and buy a record, a 45. I would have to get back in the apartment the same way I got out. Wendy always thought I was in my room. I would turn the radio on while I was gone and hoped that would keep her from wanting to come in. She knew I didn't like her to come in my room when I was listening to music or reading. Luckily, I never got caught. My friend would always call me later on in the evening to make sure I didn't get caught or get in any trouble.

Another boy, Steve, would call me on the weekends at night, when Wendy and James were at work. He was older, about fourteen or fifteen. He told me that he had an older friend who wanted to meet me. He said he had a car and would be around on the weekend. He asked me if I wanted to meet him. I told him that I did and would call him to let him know when I would be able to get out of the apartment.

It was a Saturday afternoon. Ann and I were going to go shopping together. I called Steve to tell him I would meet with him and his friend before Ann and I went shopping. The man, maybe 40 years old, drove a tan car. I could see him from a distance. He wore thick glasses.

her friend!

By looking at him I decided I didn't want to meet him. "I don't want to meet that man. He looks creepy."

"Oh, come on. We can go riding around with him. Some other girls from school know him and they go with him sometimes." Steve was tugging at my arm to go with him.

"No! I don't want to," I yelled at him. I pulled away, then ran off.

After that I would no longer talk to Steve on the phone. I would often see the man in the tan car when I was out but would quickly run away.

My foster parents would have friends over on occasion when they weren't working at the hotel. I liked talking to the people, but my foster mother would make me stay in my room while they entertained their guests. I'd find some paper and a pencil and sneak out of my room and go up to the top of the stairs, which led to the attic in the apartment. It was dark enough that no one could see me but I could still see to write. I would write stories about anything that came into my head. I'd let my imagination lead me where it wanted. One of the women guests spotted me sitting on the steps. She came up the stairs and started talking to me. She asked what I was doing with the paper and pencil. I showed her what I had written. She made such a fuss about what I had written and she called several others over to read it too. Wendy was furious that I had come out of my room and sent me back immediately to my room again without even taking the time to see what I had written. A few minutes later the lady who read my story came to my room to apologize for getting me in trouble.

I didn't like being in that foster home and I was getting more rebellious. I tried to figure ways to get moved to another foster home. I had a plan. Several friends wanted to come over one evening but I wasn't allowed to have anyone over when my foster parents weren't there. I called some friends and told them it was all right for them to come over. Wendy had not been feeling well that evening and had almost decided not to go to work but did go in. My friends arrived the same time my foster mother came back home with a terrible headache. Well, that sure took care of me getting out of that foster home. Wendy was on the phone the next day, telling Social Services what I had done and that she wanted them to find me a new home as soon as possible. In a few days the lady from social services arrived at my foster home to take me to another home.

It turned out to be an old farm out in the country. There were other foster kids there too. I learned right away what was expected of me. We all had chores to do. Every week one would have to gather the eggs from the barn or milk the cows. They had wild barn cats that lived in the barn. I have always been afraid of cats ever since the cats we had at home used to attack my feet with I was little. I was petrified at the thought of having to go in the barn to get the eggs. I would run in quickly and holler and make noises, hoping the cats would run away and hide while I gathered the eggs. I could get in the barn and back out faster than anyone else could. My foster mother always complained that when I got the eggs, we didn't get as many. She said I needed to slow down and do the job the right way or I would get grounded. When it was my turn to milk the cows, my foster sister Cindy would milk the cows for me. I would pay her to take my place. "I'll give you five dollars if you will milk the cows for me," I'd tell her. She really didn't mind milking the cows anyhow. She had milked cows and had done work on the farm since she was small. Cindy's sister had also lived there at one time. To this day, I have never milked a cow. I did watch my foster brother once just in case I would have to milk a cow at some point or if Cindy wasn't there. Several boys had come to live there so now the boys did the barn chores and Cindy and I took care of the house chores.

In the morning Cindy and I would have to make the beds, clean up the breakfast dishes and get ourselves ready for school. When we'd get home from school all the foster kids had their chores to do before getting ready for supper. After supper the dishes had to be washed, then the homework done. There wasn't much time after everything was done for any fun time, only bedtime. Five-thirty came early in the morning.

On the weekend, Cindy and I would have to clean the whole house, including changing sheets and doing the laundry, which also meant hanging the clothes outside on the clothesline. By afternoon, if everything was done, we'd have that time free to do whatever we pleased. Once in a while, I would go with a couple of friends to the next town to get pizza. There wasn't much to do living way out in the country. We didn't have a real town with shops or movies. If you blinked while going through, you missed it. We'd find someone with a car and ride around or ride up to the lake in the summer to go swimming. Some of the kids would water ski but I was too afraid to try. When Cindy got her driver's license, we'd go across the border to Campobello Island to see some boys we knew there. It was a small island that was part of Canada and was connected by only a small bridge. The boys would also come over to see us on occasion. The boys were fairly well-known in Lubec, the town where I lived, because of their size and accents. They were big boys.

In the fall, I would get up real early in the morning before any of the other kids were up. I would take a .22 rifle with me and walk out in the woods by myself. It was so peaceful and beautiful. I had a pair of deerskin boots and a jacket that I would wear. It made me feel special and powerful when I'd go in the woods wearing my boots and jacket and carrying my .22 rifle. I would see rabbits, squirrels, and sometimes even a deer or two. My foster mother didn't mind me going in the woods by myself and taking the gun. She said I was responsible enough even at my age. I was fifteen at that time. After walking in the woods for about an hour, I'd have to hurry to get back to the house to help with the morning chores and get ready for school. I so enjoyed those mornings. That was quality time for me.

School wasn't so bad there. I still felt I was behind in many things but I had more friends and was pretty popular with the teachers and the other students. I worked harder than I had before and was actually learning. I loved biology. I studied hard and got an A and an award for that class. I had a history teacher who was young and very good-looking. All the girls flirted with him and he flirted back. I liked history but he wasn't a good teacher. I didn't learn as much as I would have liked to have. He was more interested in the young girls than in teaching.

Momma did finally come to see me once while I was in that foster home. She also brought her new husband, the man who had tried to touch me, with her. She didn't stay long and I didn't see her again until I was out of foster care. My dad never came to see me. He had never been anywhere and he found it difficult to go far from home. Some of my friends had driver's licenses and several had their own cars. When one of them would get bored, I'd ask them if they would want to take me to see my dad. I visited my dad a couple of times, with the help of friends. My foster mother didn't have a problem with me going to see Dad as long as she knew the person who was taking me there.

After my brother Bobby graduated from high school he went into the Navy. He came to see me with his Navy uniform on. I was so proud and happy to see him. Meanwhile, my sister Jenny had been moved from the foster home she had been in previously and been placed in a foster home in the same town as me. We didn't see each other much, though. At that point in our lives, we had all grown apart.

One day while at school, I saw my brother David. I was shocked. I had no idea that he had been moved to a foster home in the same town also. Social Services never let us know where our family was being moved to or where they were. David had a hard time in that foster home and was very unhappy. He was being moved again and again without my knowledge. It was years later we saw each other again.

There were many kids coming and going in the foster home I was in. They even had babies living there for only a couple of months at a time and then the babies would be sent back to their real parents or adopted. If you were an older child, the chances of being adopted were slim. Dad wouldn't allow any of us to be adopted, anyway. He said he hoped one day we could all be together again at home.

Several of the foster kids had been there for years. A couple of the boys would continue to stay there even after they had gotten out of school and were eighteen. They were required to pay rent until they could find a job and find a place to live. I thought the day I turned eighteen, I would be gone from there. I would go back and live with Dad again.

Two brothers lived there in the foster home. One was out of school and had gone into the Army. The other one, named Ben, was getting ready to go in the Army. I didn't like Ben much. He didn't brush his teeth or take a shower regularly. He never had anything good to say about anyone. I thought of him as one of the foster kids though.

Ben was excited about going to Germany on his first tour. He said he had heard that he could get good stereo equipment over there at good prices. He asked Cindy if she would sign for any equipment that he sent home. She said she wouldn't, that she didn't want to be responsible for anything like that. He asked me and I agreed to help him out. It wasn't long before I received a letter from Ben saying he would be sending some equipment home in the next week. He wrote again before his shipment arrived, reminding me to sign for the shipment when it came. I did as he asked of me.

Through the next several months Ben continued to send stereo equipment home and I continued to sign for the boxes. He also wrote to see how everyone was doing at home, what the weather was like, and so on. By the time Ben had been in Germany for two years, he had a room full of equipment at the house.

He was coming home. Plans were made with my foster parents that he could stay in the foster home once again until he got a job and place to live of his own.

My foster parents, Minnie and Ed, were older. Minnie was sixty-five and her husband was seventy-three. The extra money they received from rent-payers was added income for them. They were already receiving money for fostering all the kids living there. Both of them were on Social Security as well. We were never bought any new clothes or given money to buy clothes with. We had to work in the summer to make money to buy our own clothes with.

I was seventeen when Ben got out of the Army. Ben and I talked a lot, mostly about his time over in Germany, about what it was like and the things that he saw there. I was very interested in learning about other places. I would like to go places when I was on my own. He had changed while he was away. He had some dental work done while in Germany and brushed his teeth and showered regularly. The Army had changed him for the better.

Several months had gone by since Ben had been discharged from the Army and he was still staying there. His brother had gotten out before him but was staying with some friends. Ben's brother could no longer stay where he had been staying so Minnie let him move into the foster home. He also had to pay rent to stay there. Cindy had already turned eighteen and had moved out and gotten married.

At this time I was dating a man who was also in the military but was stationed in California. I didn't see much of him, being so far away, but he did manage to get home more often than most did because his mom was very ill. Steve, my boyfriend, got to come home on leave. His mom became very sick and had to be hospitalized. I was thrilled that I would get to see him, although I was sorry that his mother was so sick. We had plans to see each other the first evening that he was to be home. Steve called me as soon as he got home and said he would be right there to pick me up. It was only about a ten-minute drive from his house so it didn't take long before he was there. We went out for pizza, talked a while, and then he gave me a diamond ring. Then he took me home, saying he needed to go see his family.

I was beside myself with happiness about the ring. I showed the ring to my foster mother but she wasn't very happy for me. She said, "You could do a lot better." I knocked on Ben's bedroom door to show him my ring. He didn't seem pleased either. I went in my bedroom to read a book. My foster dad had already gone to bed. He always went to bed early. I heard loud voices coming from Ben and his brother's bedroom. I felt they were being too noisy, especially since my foster dad was sleeping in the next room. I had to go downstairs to use the bathroom. We only had one bathroom in the house. I put my robe on and headed for the stairs. While going down the stairs, my foster mom was on her way up to bed. Shortly I was on my way back up the stairs to my bedroom, when Ben's bedroom door opened and he pulled me in the room.

I tried to make light of it, even though he frightened me, by laughing and saying, "I need to go to bed." Both the brothers were drinking whiskey, had music playing loudly, and were using foul language as they spoke. Ben was grabbing and pulling at me while calling me bitch and using other foul language. Each time he called me a name or held me stronger, his brother laughed. I tried to yell out for help several times, but no one came to help me. Ben had his hands around my neck and had pinned me on the bed. He kept grabbing my arms and shaking me. He was hurting me. I was afraid he would try to rape me. His breath in my face reeked of alcohol. It was making me feel sick to my stomach. After what seemed like an eternity, I got loose from him and ran out of their bedroom to my room and turned off the light.

There was no lock on my door, so I tried to put a chair under the doorknob in hopes that would keep Ben out if he came for me again. I was still afraid that he could get in my room. Some of the older houses had passageways that went from one room to another behind the old fireplaces like ours did. I kept thinking I heard someone coming through the passage. I was afraid to go outside the room, but afraid to stay there too. I got dressed quickly and tiptoed downstairs and slipped out the door. I ran across the yard and onto the road. I continued to run until the house was no longer in my sight. I felt as if I would never get to Steve's house, but finally I did. I knew I was hurt but didn't realize how badly the bruises were that had been inflicted on me. Now I could see the damage that he had done to my body.

Steve wasn't at home. He had gone out drinking with some buddies, or so I was told. Steve didn't come home until five a.m. He was in no condition to help me with my problem. I had stayed up all night with Steve's dad, waiting for him to get home. I told Steve what had happened and showed him my bruises. He said we would handle this later, after he had gotten some sleep.

A few hours later, I convinced Steve to take me back to the house. I needed moral support from him. I had hoped that with him there my foster mother would know that I was telling the truth and would take care of it. Minnie didn't seem as though she was surprised or upset at all. She said she would talk to Ben about it later. Ben was just coming down the stairs at that time. She asked him why he had done this to me and his reply was, "I don't know what you're talking about." He then walked out the door. Steve said very little to anyone. Steve left and went back home.

I couldn't believe that Steve had left me there. I couldn't believe this monster was getting away with doing this to me. I was hurt and tired. I didn't have anyone to help me.

Minnie told me that she felt that I needed to be moved to another foster home. She said it just wasn't working out for me to stay there any longer. I asked her to please call Social Services so I could be moved that day. Even if it was a temporary home, I didn't care. I was afraid to stay there another night. "It can wait until tomorrow. I've got things to do today," Minnie told me.

I called a friend, Alfred, to ask if he would take me to my dad's house that day. I explained what had happened. He said he would but I couldn't tell anyone who had taken me there. I agreed and I packed a few items in a bag and went out the front door, when I felt it was safe to leave and when no one was around. Alfred picked me up out of sight of the house. I felt so relieved but was still was worried that someone would find me missing and come looking for me. We were almost at my dad's house when an officer pulled us over. The officer told Alfred, "If you don't have her back to the foster home in the next twelve hours, I'll have you arrested for kidnapping." This was turning out to be a real bad day. What options did we have?

When we returned to my foster home, Alfred dropped me off at the driveway. As I walked reluctantly up the driveway I saw an unfamiliar car. It was one of the social workers. I went in the house.

"Decided to come back, huh?" Minnie asked sarcastically.

The social worker was sitting in a chair in the kitchen. "I've found you a home. You will be going there in the morning. I'll be here to pick you up about eight thirty, so be ready."

Minnie went out of the kitchen so I took the opportunity to ask the social worker if I could talk to her. "I want to press charges against Ben. I was told that I could."

"Well," she said, "we can talk about that tomorrow on the way to your new home."

I avoided talking to anyone as much as possible that evening. I went in my room and packed my things. I thought of leaving again to avoid having to stay there again that night. I would be eighteen in a few months. I thought no one would bother to find me for only a couple of months. I kept the chair up against the door and went out only long enough to go downstairs to the bathroom. I didn't feel like eating supper. First of all, I wasn't hungry, and secondly, I didn't want to be anywhere near any of those people who'd hurt me and turned their backs on me.

lived there for ~~ecked~~ how long?

The next morning the social worker arrived and I was off to a new foster home. I didn't say good-bye to anyone; I just got in the car. This was a different worker who took me to my new home. I told her that I needed to talk to someone about what happened and about filing charges against the man who abused me. She said she would talk to someone at the office when she got back there and get back in touch with me. I never heard from anyone about it again.

My new foster parents, Wade and Marty Beal, and their children were great. They had four children of their own and one they were adopting. She was mentally handicapped but she was sweet as could be. She was a very pretty little girl of three. Wade would let me make my own decisions, trusting my judgment. The first week I was there, I went to a dance just up the street from the home. I asked Wade, "What time should I be home?"

He said, "Use your own judgment, but I prefer that everyone be in the house by the time I get home from working the night shift." He was retired military but he still worked a regular job.

Marty was happy-go-lucky and loved kids. She had gotten a perm for the first time and asked me, "What do you do with this?" I laughed; not at her, but at the way she looked. She had washed it, and when it dried she brushed it out. She looked like she had four times as much hair as before.

"Just use a pick on it after it dries. Don't brush it out. You can set it with curlers if you want to."

"I kind of like it this way, don't you?" She burst out laughing also.

Katie, their youngest daughter, was a good girl. We did have words a couple of times but nothing much. We had gotten into an argument over something and Katie had said something about it to her dad. He ignored both of us and told us to come down for supper. He treated all the kids living there the same. He didn't take sides just because they were his kids. Both the boys were good boys too. I liked living there and wished that I had been able to live there from the time I had gone into foster care.

I never went back to school. I didn't want to start school again in a new area and I no longer wanted to be in foster care. Wade and Marty tried talking me into going back but I just couldn't bring myself to do so.

I sent Steve's ring back to his dad to give back to Steve. I felt that I accepted the ring in haste, not knowing what kind of man he was. I had found out that during the time I was being abused in my home, Steve was out with another woman.

It was October. I would be eighteen in a few days. I liked my foster home and parents but was ready to leave. I would be free. A couple of days before my birthday, Wade asked me where I would go when I left. "Home to stay with my dad," I told him.

He said, "If you want, you can leave tomorrow. A couple of days won't make any difference." I flew up the stairs and started packing. I called my friend, Alfred, to tell him the good news and asked if he would pick me up in the morning. He said he would be there. Finally, I would be free and on my own.

Chapter 4

Freedom

It was difficult to sleep knowing I would be leaving in the morning. I would fall asleep briefly but keep waking up. Each time I woke, I would look at the clock to see what time it was. I could hardly wait until daylight so I could get up and call my friend to come pick me up.

It was daylight. I got out of bed and quietly went in the bathroom down the hall. I washed my face, brushed my teeth and hair and looked in the mirror at myself. I smiled and said to myself, "You're gonna be free!"

Wade, Marty and their children were all still asleep. I went downstairs and called my friend to come pick me up. He said he would be there shortly. By the time Alfred arrived to pick me up Wade and Marty had gotten up. I said my good-byes and thanked them for letting me live in their home. I promised to come back to visit soon.

My dad was happy to see me and asked, "How long you down for?" He didn't realize that I was now eighteen, or would be in a couple of days.

"I'll be eighteen in a couple days, Dad. Can I stay here for a while until I get a job and get my own place?" I wanted to know. I planned to get a job, maybe at the local sardine factory. I didn't have a driver's license yet and had no car, but I figured I could find a ride with someone who worked there at the factory, or maybe Dad could take me to work.

"Yeah, guess you can. You'll have to sleep on the couch. Bobby's in the bedroom back there." Bobby had gotten out of the Navy early with a medical discharge. Dad didn't seem as excited to see me as I thought he should, but maybe he just wasn't expecting to have another person around. Dad went on to say, "Bobby stays here some of the time, if he's not out yahooing all night."

I waited a few days before I went to the factory to see if they were hiring. I had to have a couple of days to feel the freedom, with no one telling me what to do.

In October, it's already cold but very beautiful in Maine. I knew I needed to get over to the factory to check on work before they slowed down for the year. I had to make some money to hold on to for the winter when there was no work. I walked over to the factory in Southwest Harbor to apply for a job. It was about ten miles from Dad's house. My hands and feet were numb from the cold by the time I got to the factory. I asked to see the manager.

"Hi, I'm one of Floyd's daughters. Floyd Farley. I was wondering if you were hiring. I need a job." I had my fingers crossed and prayed that he would say yes.

"We're not real busy now. You may not get forty hours every week. Got to give the women who have been here a long time the time first." I was willing to take anything, even if only minimum amount of hours. "Be here in the morning at seven if you want to work."

I was eager. "I'll be here." While I was at the factory, I saw a girl whom I had gone to school with when I had lived at home years before. I went over to where she was working. She looked up and recognized me.

"Hi, Diane. Here to see your dad?"

"I'm gonna stay with Dad for awhile until I can get my own place. I got a job here starting tomorrow. I need a ride to work though. Do you drive by the house on your way here in the morning?" I asked her, crossing my fingers again. She said she did and would stop to pick me up. "Thanks. See ya in the morning then." This was great. I had been on my own only a few days and already had a job.

When I left the factory, I walked to town, another mile if that. I went in the local bar to get a Coke and was hoping I might see some familiar faces. All faces were faces of strangers. After all, it had been six years. I left the bar and walked back home.

Dad arrived home with some beefsteak. Dad called any kind of steak that was beef beefsteak. Dad liked his steak fried. He would fry it in a pan on the stove, add some water, butter, salt and pepper and thicken the water with flour to make gravy. I peeled some potatoes to boil for mashed potatoes. Dad wasn't wild about vegetables but liked his bread. Dad would say, "That's all you need to eat, meat and potatoes. Don't need all that fancy stuff." Dad never was that particular about what he had to eat as long as it filled him up, but through the years of living alone, he had gotten a bit more particular. If I made spaghetti, he'd complain and tell me straight out, "I don't like that goulash." He had gotten more set in his ways and did things his way and didn't want anyone to try to change it.

I asked Dad, "Dad, why haven't you ever gotten running water?"

He said, "I got running water. I go to the well with a bucket and run up to the house with it." Then he'd laugh. It was hard for me to get used to not having running water again. Not having a hot shower and having to go to the outhouse once again were not ideal living conditions. Dad took me to the Laundromat instead of me having to wash clothes with the old wringer washer that we used when we were kids. He said it was too much work to have to carry all that water up to the house. Male Interaction

Alfred came down to see me sometimes, mostly on the weekend. He would take me to a cheap motel so I could shower properly. We would eat out at some inexpensive restaurant. Alfred was separated from his wife. He was ten years older than me and he had two young daughters. I didn't date except when Alfred came down. I rarely went anywhere. No car, no money, and nowhere to go day after day became monotonous. I walked when I had nothing to do, even in the cold. I would go to see my sister Angie. She still lived in the same foster home.

Bobby wasn't always there to eat supper. It might be midnight before he came in. He said he couldn't get along with Dad. He said Dad was always on his case about something. Didn't matter what he did, Dad didn't approve. Bobby worked at the factory too, helping to unload the fish boats when they came in. During the winter, of course, like most places there in the area, there was no work. Dad could collect unemployment until the factories got busy again in the early spring.

Bobby and I would sit around the house and play cards when neither of us was working. Bobby taught me how to play solitaire and we would play rummy. If we had some change, we'd go over to town in the early evening to the bar and have a couple of beers. Beer was only ten cents a glass. I would sip on that beer a long time so I wouldn't have to go back home. I dreaded the walk back home and hoped that we would be lucky enough to get a ride. Bobby didn't always walk back home with me. He would take off with some guys if he got the chance to go somewhere with them. It was scary walking at night, especially walking down Long Hill. There were no houses for miles, only dense woods. I would run as much as possible to get past the stretch of road that was so dark. I knew once I got passed the hill the little grocery store was there. I felt safe then; from the store to the house wasn't very far.

By now most of my friends and people I had known growing up were either married or had moved away. Things weren't like I imagined them to be. It wasn't like the happy times growing up. I wrote to my cousin who now lived in Connecticut to see if there were any jobs available there. I thought maybe I could get a job and stay with him. He wrote back, saying, "There are jobs here, but without a car you'd have to take a bus." He didn't sound at all encouraging about me moving there. I really wanted to get my license but had no one to teach me. My brother had no car either. Dad couldn't teach me. He got too nervous when someone else was behind the wheel, he said.

David had turned eighteen and had moved back in town. I didn't see much of him but saw him out somewhere occasionally. When I did see him, he was usually with a group of guys. We hadn't seen much of each other in the past few years and had grown apart. We were now more like strangers.

It's spring! The factories are starting up again. It's time to go back to work and make a little money again. I smelled so bad from the fish after working all day. I hated the smell. It was a job and about the only thing available in this town so I didn't have much choice if I wanted to work. I could have gotten a job as a chambermaid at one of the motels in Bar Harbor if I'd had a way to get there.

The girl I had been riding with quit work at the factory so I had no ride to work anymore. I started walking to work. Sometimes I would get rides from people who worked there or someone just going that way. Dad would take me to work when he could. He was working at the other factory in Bass Harbor so it wasn't easy for him to get us both to work on time. Having worked there the year before, I would get more work than someone who had just started work that spring. Most weeks, though, the factory wouldn't get enough fish to keep all the workers busy. Sometimes I would I only be able to work a couple of days.

Alfred's wife was trying to get him to come back home. She was aware that Alfred and I were seeing each other. Alfred would lie to me. I never knew when he was telling the truth about anything. He'd tell me he wasn't staying at home with his wife but I would find he was. When I found out he was staying there when he wasn't seeing me, he'd say, "It's only because of my girls. They wanted me to stay there with them. They miss their dad. I sleep on the couch, not with her." I didn't want to see Alfred anymore but he kept coming around trying to see me.

I dreamed of how I could get away from there and go to a big city or somewhere to get a real job. I felt trapped. It was suggested by Alfred's wife that maybe I should go stay with my mom for a while to get away. She wanted Alfred to come home, and with me out of the picture she'd have a chance to get him back. I thought it was a good idea to leave too.

Mom lived in Brunswick, Maine, and was still married to Nelson. I knew I didn't want to be around him but felt sure he wouldn't try anything now. I hoped that she would let me stay.

I was put on a bus all alone in the middle of winter to go to Brunswick. I had never been on a bus before and it was scary traveling with strangers. When the bus arrived at Brunswick, I got off and got my luggage. I asked the ticket man if he would call me a taxi. I had money for a cab that Alfred had given me. When the taxi arrived, I gave him my mom's address. The taxi driver had to call the dispatcher for directions because he had no idea where she lived by the address I had given him. He located the house where he thought Mom lived, stopped the cab and went to the door to check to see if it was the right house or not. I saw Nelson at the door so knew it was the right house. I paid the driver, then he took my suitcase out of the trunk. I carried them inside the little house.

Momma was sitting at the kitchen table and got up when she saw me. She gave me a hug that was cold and unwelcome. Momma was hard of hearing so I had to talk loudly for her to hear me. "Hi, Momma! I want to get a job here. Can I stay here until I can get working and get my own place?"

She didn't seem very eager about the idea. "Can't stay long!" she announced.

The newspaper was delivered to the house early the next morning. I opened it to the help wanted section. They were hiring at a factory where they made children's clothing. Mom and Nelson didn't have a phone. Mom couldn't hear on the phone so Nelson said there was no reason to have one. I called from the neighbor's house to inquire about the job. They told me to come by and put in an application that day. I asked if Nelson could take me to the factory so I could put in the application for employment. I was frightened that he might try to touch me on the way there and didn't know what I would do if he did. My heart raced while on the drive to the factory. He never did try. I filled out the applications and was told they would call me to let me know if I got the job.

The next day Mom's neighbor came over to tell me that they had called from the factory and wanted me to start work as soon as possible. I asked Mom if it was alright if Nelson could take me to work until I could make other arrangements to get to work. He was a disabled veteran so he didn't work or do much of anything. Mom got upset when I asked. "He's not going to run your ass all around all the time." It really hurt me that she said that. I just wanted some help to get started. *Mean!*.

Nelson took me to work the next day. He returned that evening

66

to pick me up and take me back to their house. When I went in the house, Mom didn't even speak. She was cooking something for supper. "There's not much here. Won't get much if you eat here. Didn't know I'd be feeding anyone else," she said without even looking up. The store wasn't far away. It was cold outside and getting dark but I was hungry. I didn't want to eat there. I didn't feel welcome. I got some chips and a Coke from the store. The little money I had was running out, and a Coke and chips would have to be sufficient.

It was uncomfortable staying there and I knew Momma didn't want me there. The next day Nelson took me to work again. "Your mother's nerves are bad. She can't have you staying here. It gets on her nerves too much," he said. I didn't say anything back to Nelson. I knew I would have to go back to Dad's again.

I called Alfred and asked if he would come to Brunswick to get me and take me back to Dad's house. He was there that afternoon. "Bye, Momma," I said. She just made a grunting noise. Nelson said good-bye to me and we left.

Daddy wasn't home when I got there and the door was locked. I just hung around outside the house until he got home. "Didn't like staying with your mother?" he said when he saw me sitting on the steps.

"Her nerves are too bad for me to stay there."

Dad laughed. "Your mother's nerves have always been bad when she don't want to do something. She said her nerves were too bad to look after you kids anymore. When she left she said, 'I've taken care of these kids all these years, now it's your turn.' I don't think it's her nerves that were bad. She just didn't want to stay home."

Jenny got married. She married her foster parents' son, Perry. Jenny and Perry moved to a big old house. I think it belonged to someone in Perry's family. It hadn't been lived in for a long time. It had a wood furnace in the basement but the house was so big it was impossible to keep warm, especially with below-zero temperatures outside. Jenny said I could stay with them. I slept upstairs in one of the bedrooms. There were plenty of old, homemade quilts left there at the house. I went to bed early with nothing to do but play cards. The electricity hadn't been turned on because Jenny and Perry didn't have enough money to pay the monthly bill, let alone the deposit to get it turned on. With no electricity we couldn't watch TV or do anything that you had to have electricity for. I piled the old quilts on top of me so thick that I couldn't move or hardly breathe from the weight. My face and head would get cold so I had to cover them with the quilts too. As much as I didn't want to have anything to do with Alfred, I almost wished he would come and take me to a motel where it was warm and I could take a hot shower. I knew he was back with his wife and it wasn't right for me to ask him. He and his wife didn't live far from the old house where I was now living.

Jenny and Perry didn't stay long in that house. It just was too cold and unhealthy. Alfred came to the house to get me and take me back to Dad's again. Nomad - Nowhere to be & no one to be w/

My sister and her husband were moving again, this time to Brunswick, close to where Momma and Nelson lived. They came down to Dad's house to see Dad and ask me if I wanted to move to Brunswick with them. "Perry's got a job working on a dairy farm. He'll be working a lot of hours. You could keep me company." I thought that would be better than staying where I was. Hopefully they would get a house or apartment with running water and heat this time.

"When you going?" I wanted to know.

"Gonna leave in the morning but you got to get your things now, 'cause we'll go to Lubec for tonight and won't be back here."

The apartment did have running water and heat. Jenny, Perry and I played cards to pass the time. Perry was working and was gone a lot at the beginning. Jenny wanted a baby. She couldn't get pregnant right away and they started to worry. Finally, she did get pregnant. They were excited. Jenny went to see Mom while living there but I only did when I was with Jenny. They didn't stay long in Brunswick before moving back to Lubec again.

Perry had a job working on a farm when Hank was born. He was a beautiful baby. I would feed him when Jenny would let me. She would put him to bed and when he would cry, I would go in and gently rub his back until he would fall asleep. Jenny would say to me when I'd come back in the room from getting Hank to sleep, "You're spoiling him. Who's gonna get him to sleep if you're not here? He's getting too used to that. Pretty soon he won't sleep unless someone rubs his back." I knew she was right but I didn't want him to cry.

"I can't wait till the day I get married and have a baby of my own," I told Jenny.

It was moving time again. Jenny, Perry, Hank and I were moving to a small house there in Lubec. Perry was logging now. Jenny had planned to start a job soon, working the night shift. She said I would have to baby-sit if I wanted to continue to stay there. Jenny didn't work long. I decided to move back with Dad again.

Alfred didn't come around much anymore. I started going out more in the evenings and even dated a couple times. I would even walk over to the bar by myself just to get out of the house. One night while in the bar drinking a beer, a man whom I had never seen before came over to my table and said, "Hello, I'm Russell." I was thankful that the bar was dimly lit because I know that my face must have turned a brilliant red from blushing.

"Hi." That was all that I could manage to get out of my mouth. I was so nervous. Russell was tall, dark and handsome, with deep blue eyes. I found it hard to believe he was actually talking to me.

"Can I buy you a drink?" he said as he sat down at the table.

"Sure." He was there with some buddies from the Coast Guard base. The base was just down the road. He talked to me off and on while talking to his buddies. Bobby came over to the table and saw that I had met someone.

"Diane, I'm leaving," he told me. "A bunch of the guys are going to Bar Harbor so I'm riding with 'em." That meant I would have to walk home by myself again. I finished my beer and got up to leave. I didn't want to be out walking too late at night by myself.

"Hey, where you going, Diane? It's still early."

"I need to get home before it gets too much later. It's scary walking home in the dark alone." I really didn't want to blow this chance with this beautiful man but I knew I should leave.

Russell replied quickly, "I'll give you a ride home. We can have another beer then get out of this place, okay?" It sure was okay with me.

trusting

When we got to Dad's house and before I could get out of the car, Russell asked me, "Meet me there at the bar tomorrow night?" I couldn't believe this gorgeous man was asking me out.

"What time do you want me to be there?"

"Seven," Russell said.

The fact that he was so handsome, and that he had seen where I lived, made me wonder if he would show up at the bar at all. He had to know that living in the little run-down house, I was from a poor family.

I was there at the bar early. Even though it was cold out, my hands were sweating. I was worried that he wouldn't show up but also nervous about seeing him again. He was there right at seven. I didn't know what to say or how to act with this man. I was afraid to say anything, thinking it may be the wrong thing and turn him away.

We had a couple of beers and talked and then Russell made the suggestion, "How 'bout we get out of here. We could take a ride up around the lake or somewhere." I was eager to leave myself.

"I'm ready to go."

We rode up around the lake area. We sat in the car and talked about our families, among other things. Russell also had been in foster homes. His mother had been a nurse and had died from taking a medication that had a deadly reaction. The kids were young when they lost their mom. There were seven kids in his family, only one fewer than my family. His dad died not long after his mom, from cancer. The children had stayed in contact with each other through the years, unlike my family.

The moon was casting a radiance of light over the lake, the water reflecting the stars brilliantly shining in the sky. We got out of the car to walk around on the lake's edge and listen to the water gently washing up on the rocks. Romance was definitely in the air. Russell gently pulled me close.

"This is beautiful, isn't it?"

"Sure is," I said as I looked at the lake.

"You're beautiful too," Russell said as he found my mouth and kissed me.

That evening when he took me home, we made plans to go out the next evening. We continued to see each other regularly. Russell wanted to get an apartment and live off base. He asked me to move in with him. We had been seeing each other for several months now. He said he didn't make much money so any apartment he could get wouldn't be anything out of the ordinary. I was still working as much as possible at the fish factory so my small paycheck might help to pay bills. He got us an efficiency apartment close to the base so he could walk to work if he had to. We moved into the furnished apartment as soon as the lease was signed.

Alfred found out that I had met someone else. He had been trying to find me. He came up to the apartment and wanted me to let him in to talk. I refused. I told Russell who he was and that he had come by. It didn't take much from Russell to discourage Alfred from bothering me. I had heard that he left his wife. I never heard or saw him again.

Dad came over to visit us frequently. If Russell happened to be drinking a beer when Dad came over he would pour the beer into a colored plastic cup so Dad wouldn't know it was beer. Daddy wouldn't have said anything but Russell said it was out of respect for my dad.

Russell and I would go visit Dad sometimes too. I got Dad to play badminton with us one day out in the backyard. Daddy went to hit the birdie, tripped, fell backward, and turned a somersault. I started laughing. It was so funny. I didn't know if Dad was hurt or not, but it was just so awkward that it was funny. He acted as if he was mad at first but then started laughing too.

I was no longer working at the factory. Russell couldn't stand the fish smell on my clothes.

"Can't stand that stinky fish. Go change and hang 'em outside." I hung them over the rail of the little balcony we had outside the apartment.

"Your fingers are always sore, swollen and bleeding. You need to quit that job. You don't make enough to put up with all this."

I kept my fingers taped up with white tape but the scissors were so sharp, if you missed the fish, it would cut through the tape and cut your finger. Some women had lost fingertips from packing sardines. It was a hard job anyhow to stand on your feet all day, smell that fish, and pack that fish in cans. It hardly seemed worth it but I liked working. I liked having some money to help with the bills.

My brother Bobby had moved to the campground at Seawall. He had shower rooms there and flush toilets to use. He would stay there at the campground during the summer and move back with Dad in the winter. When he lived with Dad he would come over to the apartment about once a week and ask if he could take a shower. Russell let him take showers there for a while but said Bobby needed to do more for himself and that he couldn't continue to let him come over to take showers. That upset me but I went along with what he said. After all, he was now paying all the bills. I knew what it was like not having the opportunity to better yourself even if you wanted to.

Russell and I went to Vermont about one weekend out of the month when he didn't have duty on base. His foster parents lived there and so did the kids he grew up with in that foster home. They didn't allow us to sleep in the same room together even though they knew we lived together. Russell's foster father was a minister. They didn't approve of our living arrangements and often talked to us about getting married. We had been living together for almost a year now. We decided that we wanted to get married but didn't want to start a family yet. We would wait to see how things went after he got out of service.

72

Chapter 5

Getting Married

We made plans to be married in November 1973. Russell's cousin who lived in New Hampshire helped with the wedding plans. She made arrangements for us to be married in a quaint chapel in New Hampshire. We invited a limited number of friends and mostly immediate family. We would have a small reception at his cousin's house after the wedding. For our honeymoon we were going to Montréal for a week.

The wedding went well except for my being so nervous. We didn't stay long at the reception before we were off to Montréal. We stayed in a quiet, cozy little motel way out in the country in the White Mountains. All the leaves were off the trees and even in the dark of night you could see the white birch trees. When we got to Montréal we were lost so we stopped to ask directions. None of the Canadians that we spoke with understood English, only French. We were frustrated at getting no directions so we left there to go back home. We did stop on the way home to do some sight-seeing and enjoy some of the spectacular country.

When Russell had weekend duty on the base I would go visit him in the evening. He would have to go out on sunset patrol in one of the patrol boats. He was an engineman, and when the Coast Guardsmen went out on patrols they had to have a full crew. I would often go out on patrol with them.

The sun setting on the ocean in the quiet of the early evening was breathtaking. Other private boats were out cruising and enjoying the fantastic view on the sea. Fishermen were coming in after a long day of fishing and hauling traps. The sailboats' sails rippled in the light southeastern wind and the captains waved a friendly hello as we passed by.

Russell's tour of duty was almost up. We had to make a decision whether or not he would stay in the Coast Guard or get out and be a civilian. We went to talk to the Coast Guard recruiter to find out where Russell might be shipped if he stayed in. They told us that it was inevitable that he would go out on a ship, probably out of Boston, Massachusetts. He would be out for six months. Because we were newlyweds, we didn't want to be separated. We then went to talk to the Army recruiter who was right next door.

"I can give you a year in Colorado if you go in as a cook, and chances are, the rest of the time, another stateside duty."

It was frightening to think of going so far away from home but we decided that would be our best choice. Russell signed the papers to go in the Army as a cook. He liked to cook and had hoped that someday we could open our own little restaurant.

"This will give me some experience for when we get our own restaurant," he'd say.

The day came when his time was up in the Coast Guard. He had thirty days before we had to be in Colorado. The moving truck arrived to pack and load up what few things we had to move. We didn't have to worry about packing ourselves, only what we needed for the trip to Colorado.

Russell had to go to basic training in North Carolina before we would go to Colorado. We drove to New Hampshire to his cousin's house. He and his cousin, Dana, took me to Logan Airport and sent me to his sister Rhonda's house in Ohio. I would stay there until he finished basic. After basic training he flew back to New Hampshire to get our car and drive to Ohio. We visited a couple of days and then headed for Colorado.

I had never seen such beauty. We drove eight or nine hours a day. I had never seen the oil diggers before and didn't know what they were when I saw them. In Oklahoma there were oil diggers everywhere. Kansas was so flat that you could see for miles. I was enjoying the trip. I got to see things that I had only heard or read about.

It was the last day of traveling. We were in Colorado. The wind was blowing tumbleweeds across the road in front of us. You could see trash blown up against the fences along the road. We ran over a big snake and Russell said he believed it was a rattler. We drove for miles with nothing in sight except fields of emptiness. I got a lonesome feeling inside of me. We could have been in another country and it wouldn't have felt any different.

We got into Colorado Springs early that day. Now we had to find a place to live. Russell stopped to ask at a grocery store if they knew of any apartments nearby that were available for rent. The man gave us directions to an apartment complex close by. We had no problem getting a one bedroom and moved in as soon as the papers were signed. Russell went to the base to report in.

The altitude in Colorado was not what I was used to. I had a nosebleed the first night there. I had to learn to cook and bake with high altitude recipes.

Our bedroom window was located on the west side of the building. We had a great view of the Rocky Mountains. Russell had to get up at 4:30 a.m. to go in to work. I would get up with him to have coffee and make him a light breakfast. Even though it was cold outside, I would open the bedroom window just a crack to hear the coyotes howling in the mountains. It was eerie to hear them howl, but I liked to listen. It was like what you might see on *National Geographic* or *Animal Kingdom*. After Russell had left for work I would drink my coffee and look out the window for day to break. When the sun came up, it covered the side of the mountain in a magnificent array of gold. It was a wondrous sight to see.

Living in that apartment was awkward. We couldn't do much, like change the oil in the car or sit outside in the evening. We started looking for a new place. We found a duplex and moved in immediately. At the new place we even had a small yard. It was nice to able to sit outside or wash the car if you wanted to.

In the summer we would get a tremendous amount of rainfall with hail about the same time every day for a week. Sometimes our apartment would get flooded with water up to two inches in only minutes. There were drains built in the cement pad at the bottom of the steps leading down into the apartment. With the amount of rain that fell so quickly the drains couldn't handle it. The water would come in under the door of our apartment and flood it. The landlord would come down to our apartment with a pump to help remove the water. During the pumping procedure the door would be open. Salamanders would come in along with the water. They had been forced down the steps by the powerful force of the rain. It was strange to have creatures in the apartment. After the water was all removed, we would still find a salamander or two that got overlooked.

We often went trout fishing and camping in the mountains. There were streams to fish in everywhere. Most people would camp out in a secluded area by a stream and fish for days. Russell said that for my birthday we would do something special.

"You want to go camping up in the mountains. We could rent a pop-up camper; take some fishing poles and fish."

I was delighted. "Maybe we could stop at Santa's Workshop on the way. I've always wanted to go in there."

"Sounds fun to me. Yeah, let's do that."

We would find a nice quiet place up around Cripple Creek to set up the camper and fish. It was warm during the day. We had heat from the lamps but didn't think we would need more than that. It got cold during the night. In the morning I was ready to go outside and make a fire to get warm and cook breakfast. A blanket of snow had fallen during the night. The sun shining on the new snow was blinding but awesome. I made bacon, eggs and fried potatoes for breakfast. I put bread on the grate to make toast. I always ate too much when I went camping. Food tastes so good cooking out in the open.

We went downstream to try catching trout. We could never quite get the hang of fly fishing. Needless to say, we didn't have fish for supper but we had fun trying.

On another weekend, we took a trip to New Mexico. New Mexico has more of a rocky terrain than Colorado. I had never had real Mexican food. We stopped in a restaurant and had lunch. The food was so spicy that I could only eat a small portion of it. It was good though. We stayed at a campground overnight and drove back home the next day.

Christmas in Colorado was lonesome. We had no family close by and we only knew a few people. Most of the couples we knew had children so they wanted to spend their time at Christmas with family. Rhonda and her husband, Bob, and another couple were going to Steamboat Springs for Christmas to go skiing. Rhonda called us and said that if we would drive up to the lodge to get her on Christmas Eve day, she would come down to our apartment and spend Christmas Eve with us. We would take her back on Christmas day.

The roads going up through the mountains were clear with just a few snowdrifts and icy spots here and there. The snow-covered mountains looked like picture postcards. It was a winter wonderland. From the mountains you could see the steam from the trains running on the tracks below.

In the morning we woke early to open gifts—we got extra gifts for Rhonda so she would have more to open—then I made my famous egg, ham and cheese casserole. It is an easy dish to make without having a lot of pans and dishes to clean up afterward. I packed us a few things, warm clothes and some cosmetics. As before the drive up to the lodge was pleasant. Rhonda drove some of the way so I got stuck sitting in the backseat of the car. I didn't have a license yet. We stayed at the lodge that night. I spent more time alone there because Russell hung around his sister most of the time. We had to sleep in the same room with his sister and husband on the floor because there were only two bedrooms and both were occupied. There was a couch in the living room but another man had come with them to ski so he slept on the couch.

Cleaning the apartment during the day didn't take long and I was tired of watching TV. I would cook, bake and eat. I was gaining weight and getting depressed.

"I want a baby. Let's not wait until you get out of the army. I have all this time right now with nothing to do except get fat." Russell agreed not to wait any longer either. I went to the doctor. He said I was fine and saw no reason I couldn't get pregnant. I went off the pill.

Two months went by. Three months. Back to the doctor I went. "I'm not pregnant yet. It's been three months." The doctor didn't seem too concerned. He said, "Sometimes after being on the pill, it takes longer. Give it some more time."

We did the temperature thing. When my temperature went up, we had to make love. Six months and not pregnant yet. The doctor ran some routine tests and things seemed to be normal. Russell had to have a sperm check as well to be sure he was all right. The next month, the doctor scheduled me to have a test done that would tell if my fallopian tubes were blocked or not. The test was very painful. The doctor would inject dye up through the uterus and see if it would come through the fallopian tubes. I was cramped for hours. The doctor said my chances of getting pregnant were only 50 percent; I had a blockage on one side.

After that when we would go to the grocery store or to department store and I would see pregnant women, I would cry. I couldn't believe I couldn't have a child of my own. I had such an empty place inside me. It just wasn't fair.

On Friday nights there would be a party at a hall near where we lived. It was all military people. If you wanted to drink liquor, you had to bring your own bottle. You could buy mixers for liquor and soft drinks along with beer. We went out a couple times a month. I didn't know many people and it was always uncomfortable being there. We both would drink too much and get into arguments about stupid things.

I felt I wasn't worthy of Russell. I was getting fat and I felt ugly. Now I couldn't even give him a child. I was so unhappy. I hoped for the time to be up there so we could go back home to see family before the next assignment.

I still wanted to get my driver's license so I could get a job while living there. Russell tried to teach me to drive but he was so impatient we gave it up. We had lived in Colorado for almost a year now. Russell got his orders. He was going to Korea. This wasn't right. He was supposed to get stateside duty. Russell tried to get out of the orders and get a stateside duty but the Army said he had to go.

I would go back to New Hampshire to live. Dana knew of someone who owned a tiny cottage about three miles from Hampton Beach. The woman who owned it said she would rent it to me cheap while Russell was overseas. Dana would be there to help me and take me places I needed to go.

Russell left for Korea. I was left alone. Our car was left with me but what good was it if I couldn't drive it? One day after I was complaining that I was still stuck with nothing to do, Dana said, "I'll teach you to drive."

She was very patient and I got my license soon after. I got a job at a Howard Johnson's motel. I became friends with a girl named April who also worked there. We would drive around, each in our own cars, and follow each other to the beach. I also became good friends with the chef at Howard Johnson's, Jim. He was older but I liked to talk to him. He read a lot of books, newspapers, magazines and any type of reading material that he could get his hands on. April and I would be out doing something on the weekend and ride over to Jim's house to visit with him and sometimes we would get fresh doughnuts to take him.

My sister Shari had gotten married and was living in Rhode Island. She and Doug had a newborn baby. Her name was Lori. I wanted to go down to see her and the baby but was too afraid to drive in all that traffic. Jim offered to take me to my sister's house on Friday evening and come back on Sunday to pick me up. I was really happy that he was willing to take me there.

It was nice to see my sister. Lori was so tiny and I told Shari, "She looks like a little frog with that fat little belly." She was such a beautiful baby.

Shari and Doug were having problems in their marriage. Shari came up to the cottage and was really upset. She didn't know what she was going to do. I took her downtown to see if she could get some assistance for her and the baby. She and the baby could stay with me. She was so emotional and going through such a hard time, she decided it would be best to go back to Rhode Island with Doug.

I wanted a dog. A dog would be good company for me. I got a three-month-old male black Lab while Russell was in Korea. He was full of energy. He was tied in the front yard and had a doghouse. I kept

79

him in the house during the day while I was at work. I didn't know much about that breed of dog and all the attention that he required. I had never had a dog before. I went to work one day and when I came home, he had chewed all the electrical cords off everything that he could get to. He had managed to unplug them from the wall first though. I was happy that Dana's husband, Micky, was an electrician and was able to replace the cords.

Momma was having some problems with Nelson. They weren't getting along. Mom got Nelson to bring her to my cottage to see me. He sat in the car while Mom came in. Mom asked, "Can I stay with you until I can find a place of my own?" My first instinct was to say no, but she was my mother and it was hard for me to say no to her.

"You can stay but I don't want Nelson hanging around."

Momma looked at me and said, "Well, if that's the way you are, you're no daughter of mine!" and she left.

My weight was at a horrible 132 pounds. I joined a weight club called TOPS. TOPS stood for Take Off Pounds Sensibly. I took off the weight in no time. Working at the motel helped with the exercise and I started running. I would run up and down the driveway at the cottage. I would get a charm if I took off the most pounds that week. I had a full bracelet of charms that I received from the weight club.

Several months had gone by and I missed Russell. I wanted him to come home. I knew he would be proud of me losing weight, driving, and having a job. I got a new job at a plant called Data General. They trained me for two weeks, then I went on afternoon shift. I liked the job. After work some of the workers would go to a local bar not far from the plant. I felt I was hanging around the wrong people and drinking too much, but I missed Russell and wanted to be with people and not alone.

Russell got home from Korea earlier than originally planned. He was to come home for 30 days and go to California to finish out his two years with the Army. Russell's brother found out that he was coming home. Ron called me from Massachusetts, where he lived, and said, "We're on out way down there." I didn't have time to ask him if he would wait and come down later. I felt that Russell and I needed some time alone first. Dana and I went to the airport to pick

Russell up. It was a cool hello for us both. There had been so many changes, especially with me. There had been too many months of separation.

Ron, his wife and two girls were already at the cottage. Everyone hugged, and then the beer came out. "We got to celebrate your homecoming." Ron took a big swallow of beer.

Finally Ron and his family left. We were finally alone. Where do we start? We were like strangers. We wanted to make love but neither of us could get ready. Too much had changed and we would have to get used to each other again.

It was time to leave for California.

Chapter 6

Moving Again

The moving truck arrived to pack our things for us. As before we packed our personal things that we needed for the trip. This time we had a new passenger. Pluto, my black lab, was going to California with us. He went everywhere with me so he was used to riding. Pluto went with me to visit Dad while living there at the cottage. There was a storm coming but I didn't think it would be too bad, so Pluto and I left to go to Maine. It took about four and a half hours to drive to where Dad lived from Hampton Beach. The storm got progressively worse as I continued to drive. It was snowing and icing everything. The roads were becoming slick and I could barely see past the headlights anymore. It took seven hours to get to Dad's house. I was never so happy to get off the road as I was then. Pluto never whined the whole way down there, he just slept on the backseat.

Russell suggested that we see some new scenery this time traveling out west. We would stop to see his sister Rhonda in Ohio first. We went through Nebraska, Wyoming, Utah, and then into Reno, Nevada, where we stayed the night and checked out the slot machines. We had rolls of nickels that we had saved for the slots. Nebraska had wide-open country with herds of wild animals. Buffalo herds were common to see. We stopped in Salt Lake City to see the sights. We drove through most of Nevada at night so I couldn't see much, but I could hear the coyotes howling in the darkness. It was at least sixty to seventy miles once you stopped at some little gas station before you would find another one. Planning your fuel was essential while driving through Nevada.

One of the first places we came to in Reno was a small restaurant with a gas station and big sign on the door: WE HAVE SLOTS. We walked the dog and then went inside to eat and see the slot machines. I had never seen slots and had no idea how to play them except what I had seen on T V and what I had been told from people who had played them before. It was exciting. I didn't care then if I ate or not, I just wanted to play the slots. We did eat first, though, Russell insisted. I went through the first roll of quarters in no time and didn't win anything back. I had one more roll. That was gone in a hurry also. Russell said, "It's time to go." We needed to find a place to spend the night.

"Just one more try, please?" I begged.

Russell said, "No!" so we left. We found an inexpensive motel about thirty miles away and spent the night there.

The next morning we headed for California, where we would live for the next five months. Monterey had lots of boats anchored at its wharfs and in the harbors. It looked like a nice place to live; the water and boats reminded me of home. We started looking for an apartment but couldn't find any place that would accept animals. "No dogs," is all we heard. I began to panic, thinking I may have to give up Pluto. We were unable to find a place to live. We had to stay in a motel that first night. The next day we searched again but with no luck.

After trying to figure out what we were going to do, Russell asked, "Would you want to go back to Colorado and see if we can find a place for you to stay so you can keep Pluto?" I didn't want us to be separated again but I couldn't bear the thought of giving up my dog either. We decided to drive back to Colorado and see what we could find. We found a trailer for rent in a dumpy trailer park. The rent was reasonable and I could keep Pluto. I had to do a lot of cleaning in the trailer, it was so dirty. I caught three mice a day for the first week of living there. After that the mice seemed to be gone. There wasn't much to do there by myself so I spent most of my time playing with

Pluto. I would watch the young boys walk through the trailer park carrying a dead rattlesnake over their heads several afternoons each week.

Russell would stay at the barracks on base in California and come to see me every couple of weeks. He would have to fly back and forth because I needed the car with me. That only lasted a month. We couldn't afford for him to fly back and forth that often and we didn't like being separated again. We would have to find Pluto a new home. Russell seemed to resent Pluto anyway. Russell took him to a shelter in Colorado with his registration papers. I asked Russell to give them our old address so they could give it to the person who takes him. I wanted to know where he was going. I cried for my dog. Russell knew it broke my heart to have to give him up and asked, "Do you want to go back and get him? We'll figure something else out to do." I did want to go back and get him but knew I couldn't.

We found an apartment in Santa Cruz. It was small but clean and we didn't need it for very long anyhow. Across from where we lived there were no houses and it was mostly sand, with the exception of those little weeds that had pickers on them. We didn't have much to do, and with a limited budget we couldn't afford to go out much. Playing Frisbee was something that we did regularly. I had to wear socks with my sneakers to keep the pickers from sticking in my skin. It stayed about 74 to 76 degrees in Santa Cruz all the time. Fog was heavy in the morning until about 10:00 a.m. when it would be burnt off by the sun.

I got a letter from an older couple that lived in Pueblo, Colorado. They said, "We got your Pluto the day after you left him at the shelter." They went on to say, "We love him already. He is such a good dog and very smart." I was so happy that he had a new home but I still missed him.

Rhonda said she thought sure that Russell could get a job there in Warren, Ohio, when he got out of the Army, working for Ohio Edison. His time in the Army had ended. Ohio might not be so bad. We packed again and drove to Ohio. Russell got a job working for Ohio Edison as a mechanic. He worked the afternoon shift. We stayed with Rhonda for a few weeks and then found an apartment.

The apartment was upstairs in a house that had been made into two apartments. The owner lived in the bottom apartment. Money was still a problem and the landlady offered us a good deal, saying, "If you want to clear some of the bush out in the backyard and cut down some of those small trees, I'll deduct it from your rent." Just getting started again we needed to save any money we could. We cleared brush and trees every weekend until it was finished.

Russell came home from work one day with a black lab puppy. She was three months old according to the vet. She had been running around the bowling alley for days where one of the guys Russell worked with had been bowling. She was wild and would jump up and bite me when we were outside working in the backyard. I know she was just playing, but she scared me. We named her Angel. The vet said she was purebred from what he could tell. She stayed inside the apartment most of the time. We didn't have a doghouse for her yet and no place to keep her outside. I trained her to only go in certain rooms. She wasn't allowed in the bathroom at all. She would whine when I was taking a bath and wanted to come in to see me. She rode in the car with me wherever I went unless it was to work.

I got a job at a motel cleaning rooms close to where we lived. With me working we really needed two vehicles. We were told about a white Volkswagen for sale and they weren't asking much money for it. It had no heat in it at all but I didn't have far to drive to work. I really liked my little car. We had to park it on the end of the driveway next to the hill because the parking was limited. Down below the hill was the backyard.

I was deathly sick one day after work with a stomach virus and I was running a fever of 102 degrees. I kept getting up from bed after having nightmares that someone was in the bedroom with a gun trying to shoot me. I sat in the living room for a while, not wanting to go back to bed yet. I heard a noise in the backyard. I looked out the window to see a car in the backyard. Someone was driving it around out there. I thought the fever was making me delirious and maybe I was seeing things. I felt so weak but made it back to the bedroom. "Russell, wake up! There's a car in our backyard." He looked at me like I was crazy.

"Sure is a car down there," he said to me. In the meantime, our landlady was already outside and looking down back. Russell went outside and over to stand by her. I couldn't hear what they were saying but were pointing at the hill. The girl had evidently lost control of her car, gone over the hill and was trying to get back up over the hill. Before going down over the hill she hit my little car and totaled it. Her insurance company paid for my car but it wasn't worth fixing so I had no car again.

A year had gone by and our lease was up on our apartment. We decided it was time to buy a home of our own. The home we bought needed some additional work but it was all our budget could afford at that time. Russell wanted to save every penny we made. We never went out or did anything. I quit my job at the motel and got a job working at a local bakery making pies and cakes and learning to decorate them. The baker who worked there was leaving soon; he had another job that paid more money. He taught me everything that he could before leaving the job. I liked working there. I had to open the shop early in the morning. I baked pies and cakes for the display case for customers who came in the store. After everything was put out in the display case, I would decorate cakes to customers' specifications. I took a cake decorating class to increase my knowledge. Because we only had one car, Russell would take me to work in the mornings and Rhonda would pick me up at night.

We found a Ford Torino for sale so Russell bought it for us. It sure had the power. It scared me to drive it but I soon got used to it. I had to have two hands on the wheel at all times though, just to keep it on the road.

The house we bought didn't have carpeting; it had ugly gray title in every room. One of Rhonda's friends who was well-off was replacing the carpet in her house. One room of carpet in her house would carpet two of our rooms. She hadn't had the carpet down long but just decided she wanted something different. It was gold in color and very plush. It was like brand new. Rhonda's friend gave us the carpet and we found someone to lay it for us, cheap. The next thing was wallpaper for the master bedroom.

I had already decided what I wanted for wallpaper. I wanted

something white with small flowers as a print. I had planned to get a white lace bedspread with matching curtains. I didn't know how to wallpaper but Rhonda did and she said she would help. She wanted to be in charge of picking out the paper and running the whole show. Neither Russell nor Rhonda thought I had enough intelligence to do anything. I couldn't make any decisions without checking with Rhonda to see if it was all right, as far as Russell was concerned, that is. I did get what I wanted in the wallpaper and my bedspread with matching curtains, but not without arguments from both of them.

Russell's family always wanted to run our lives, and Russell let them. I was getting tired of feeling like I couldn't do anything without first getting approval from his family. We went on vacation once a year and always went back to New England to visit family. There was always conflict with his brother because we had planned to divide our time up with my family in Maine and his brother in Massachusetts. His brother would say, "We haven't seen you for a whole year. Why do you have to go to Maine? Why don't you go there next year?" We ended up spending most of our vacation with his brother because Russell would do what his brother wanted. I usually got to have a day to see all my family.

My younger sister Angie was getting married. Her fiancé and his family lived on Swans Island, a small island off the coast of Maine. They had planned to be married in a church there. I wanted to go to the wedding. Russell didn't act like he wanted to go. "I can't get off work." He didn't have to go.

"I will go alone then."

"There's no way you are going to Maine by yourself," he replied.

I asked my girlfriend Carla if she wanted to go with me. Carla said she wanted to go but didn't know if her boyfriend, with whom she was living, would want her to. With some persuasion, he agreed to let her. She didn't drive so I had to drive the whole way myself, but she was good company. We got in Massachusetts and I heard a noise coming from the car. At first I thought maybe a tire was low or flat. We pulled over off the highway but I couldn't see anything wrong. As soon as I got to the first rest area, I pulled in to call Russell's brother for help. His wife had gone to Oklahoma to visit her family for the week and he was partying with a friend. I got directions to his house. I didn't know how to get there from where I was. On arrival at his house, he looked under the car but didn't see anything wrong either. I called Russell to tell him what had happened and where I was. He was upset and said, "I knew something like this was going to happen." Russell then added, "You're not spending the night there, are you?" His brother, Ron, got on the phone and talk to him in hope of calming him. He told Russell he would take good care of us, not to worry. We stayed the night there and started for Maine the next morning.

The car was still making a noise. We were in Hampton, New Hampshire, and I told Carla that I was getting hungry so we stopped at a McDonald's to get a biscuit to eat on the way. We didn't have much time to get to the ferry boat. We had to get there in time to catch the boat that went over to the island in time for the wedding. As I was trying to back the car out of the parking spot, the car wouldn't turn. I pulled in again and tried to back out again. The car still wouldn't turn. I got out of the car and looked underneath. I could see something hanging as if it was broken. I called Russell at his work to tell him what I seen under the car. "Guess you better call a tow truck and have them to take it someplace to get it fixed," he grumbled at me. I went across the street to a garage and asked them whom I should call. The man was very helpful and gave me a number but said he would make the call for me if I wanted him to. The tow truck was there in only a few minutes. He said Carla and I could ride in the truck to the place he was taking the car to be fixed.

The car took several hours to fix and by that time the wedding was over and it was too late to start back to Ohio. We got a room at a motel in Hampton and stayed the night there. We were up early the next morning and left for home.

When we returned to Ohio, I went up to see Russell at work to let him know we were back. He was upset with me. He said, "You will never go on a trip again without me." He kept talking about Betty. She was a divorced black girl who worked in the office there. She had been talking to Russell during the time I was gone. She was just a friend and a co-worker, he said.

Russell and I argued on a regular basis about everything. The

88

Controlling

smallest thing would trigger an argument. It was hard to say who started it because it was mainly over stupid things anyway.

I started running again and exercising all the time to keep in shape. It made me feel good. Russell didn't like it that I started trying to keep in shape again. It made him feel more insecure about our marriage and his own life. We continued to argue more and more all the time. He didn't want me to leave the house when he was at work, and if I just went to the store, he would get upset. I felt like I was in prison. I had to get permission to do everything.

The pie shop where I had been working closed down. I got a job working for an elderly couple cleaning their house and doing laundry. Margie had never had children and she was kind of out-spoken and bossy. She was a short, stout woman, sixty-five years old. John was tall, thin, and had beautiful white hair and blue eyes. He had been born in Sweden. John was eighty years old and as sweet as they come. I would clean house on Wednesdays and do laundry on Fridays. After the laundry was done on Friday, it was lunchtime. John would ask Margie, "Can Diane go get us some fish at Long John Silver's for lunch?" He loved the fish there. Margie would insist that I get lunch also and stay and eat with them. I worked for a cleaning service on the days I didn't work for Margie. I had four houses that I cleaned each week.

Things kept getting worse between Russell and me. I started seeing a counselor. I wanted Russell to go with me. Our marriage was falling apart and we needed help to save it. The counselor said one of the problems he felt we had is that I wanted and needed to grow and Russell didn't. I wanted to go forward. He liked the way things used to be before I became so independent. I wanted to learn about new things and maybe do something besides cleaning motel rooms and other people's homes the rest of my life. Russell wasn't able to accept the changes with me and suggested, "Why don't you go back to the doctor to have that test done again? Maybe they can do something else so you could get pregnant." He felt if I were able to have a child, I would be more content just being a mother and wife.

The doctors, at that time, were recommending using fertility drugs for women who had problems getting pregnant. I set up an appointment at the Cleveland Clinic with a gynecologist and Russell and I went to talk to the doctor. He didn't recommend me taking the fertility drug but to go have the test done again that I had had in Colorado. This would determine if there had been any change since the last test. He set me up to have the test done as an out-patient in our local hospital with a doctor there. He would in turn get the results from the other doctor and then we would talk. This time they found both tubes to be blocked. It was so incredibly painful, more painful than the first time. I lay on the bed at Rhonda's house for several hours, not moving from the pain and the disappointment, now with no hope of being able to ever conceive. There was nothing else that could be done for me.

It had become very uncomfortable at the house. It was like walking on eggshells. I was afraid to say or do anything; Russell was so quick to argue with me. There was no pleasing him. He complained about everything I did or didn't do. We got to the point where we would sleep in separate rooms sometimes.

I had had enough. I told Russell one evening after he got home from work, "I can't live like this anymore. I am moving out." At first he accused me of seeing someone else and then just sat on the couch with his headset on listening to country music and not talking at all. I moved out the next day. I moved in with a woman whom I knew from where I now worked. We both worked at the Best Western motel right up over the hill from her house. She had a big white house and had it decorated very nicely. She let me stay in the room that her daughter had built on to the house when she lived there. Ester said, "If you just pay utilities for the house that will be your rent."

Neither Russell nor I got an attorney. We decided to be civil and handle the divorce ourselves. I didn't take much from the house but wanted the bed and dresser. Margie had given it to us when she bought a new set. I also took my lace bedspread and curtains. I took the car that was paid off because I knew I couldn't make the payments on the other car that we had gotten after we sold the Torino.

I found someone to deliver some firewood to Ester's house for the fireplace. I had a bar set up in the room with about any kind of liquor you could want. We would get a fire going in the fireplace and have friends over to have drinks

Ester was fifty-two years old but she still liked to have a good time. She had two grown children and had grandchildren. Ester was a good-looking woman and still had a good figure for her age. Her husband had died some years before but she never remarried or even dated.

We had a big Christmas party the first Christmas I was there. We played Christmas disco music on my new stereo that I bought on sale at J. C. Penney's. I had gotten my first credit card so I put the new stereo on it. We made little sandwiches and we had snack foods. I made a Christmas cake. I decorated it up like a Christmas village with candy canes, elves, and of course Santa.

I was twenty-nine when we got our divorce three months later in Ohio. We met there at the court house and went inside together. We were divorced in only a few minutes after the judge called our case. We decided to go have lunch together and talk. We didn't hate each other, we just knew that we couldn't get along. We still talked some after that and saw each other some. Several weeks after our divorce, Russell told me he was dating Betty, the black girl from where he worked. It shouldn't have been any surprise to me, but I was shocked. He said, "Betty was there for me while I was going through our divorce."

I said, "Yeah, I bet she was." He didn't say anything else. I found out months later that Russell had been hospitalized for two weeks after our separation. He was so devastated that I left, he fell apart. The doctor said he had a chemical imbalance.

One Saturday evening Ester said, "Why don't we get dressed up and go out somewhere?" There weren't many choices of places to go dressed up. We tried to decide where we should go.

"Why don't we go up to the country bar up over the hill?" I said. They had a band playing. Maybe we would get lucky and someone would ask us to dance. We sat at a small table next to a window. There was no table service; you had to get your drinks from the bar. I went up to the bar and ordered each of us a Singapore sling. I brought our drinks to the table and we drank and talked. We soon got another drink. We had almost finished the second one when a young man about twenty-five years old came over to our table. He asked me, "Would you like to dance?

I said in reply, "Maybe later."

He continued to talk to us and then asked, "Can I buy you girls another drink?"

Ester then spoke up, "I don't know if we would have time to drink them before her dad will be here to pick us up." I did not know what she was up to, but went along. She said, "He doesn't like to have to wait if he's in a hurry to get someplace on business."

The man was all ears and then spoke again, "Your husband?" Ester nodded. He said, "What does your husband do?"

I got in on the conversation. "Oh, my dad is a construction contractor. He builds those big skyscrapers like the ones in New York City."

The man eye's got big. "Stay right there." He went to the bar and quickly brought back a drink for each of us. He continued to talk. "So, where is he now?"

Ester looked at me and then said, "He had some business in Pittsburgh, and as soon as he picks us up we are going to Cleveland. I just hope the driver doesn't get lost trying to find this little place."

"You have a driver?" the man asked, seeming impressed.

"Dad usually flies but we wanted to tag along to visit some people we had met last year at a convention in Cleveland. Dad said he would take the limo so we could go visit," I told the man. The man said he would be right back. He went to the men's room. That was our chance to escape and we took it. Don't know how much longer we could have kept him going without one of us busting out laughing. We got in Ester's car and left in a hurry. We both burst out laughing. "That was great," I said with tears rolling down my face from laughing so hard.

"Yeah, we could get in the movies." Ester was still laughing.

Ester and I liked to go up to the truck stop to have a cheeseburger and fries when we could afford to. One Tuesday evening neither of us felt like making anything there at the house to eat so we decided to go up to the truck stop. We both ordered the usual, cheeseburger and fries. Our food was ready and we were enjoying our food while talking. There were a couple of older gentlemen sitting in the booth in front of us. One of the men had dark hair and a dark complexion and was very good-looking. He looked Italian. He was trying to get Ester's attention by making little comments at things we were talking about. We were discussing who we could get, cheap, to fix the pipe that went to the shower stall in her basement. Dan, the good-looking man, stood up and said, "I can fix your pipes, miss." Ester appeared to be embarrassed and had no words to say.

The other man sitting at the booth with him spoke up, "He really can fix your pipes." I started laughing and then Dan started laughing. Ester wasn't sure what to say. She wasn't used to having a man flirting with her. Dan said if it was all right he would come to the house the next evening and take a look at that pipe. Ester wasn't sure if that was a good idea or not, not knowing the man. Before we left she felt more comfortable with him and agreed to let him look at the pipe.

Dan was there the next evening. He asked, "So where is this pipe that needs fixing?" He stood looking at Ester and chuckling.

She pointed to the basement and said, "Down there."

"You sure that's where the pipe needs fixing?" Dan questioned, playing with Ester. He went to the basement and in no time was back upstairs.

"It won't be no problem to fix and will only cost you a dinner with me."

Ester said, "I'll just pay you to fix it. How much will it be?"

"Not much, a couple of dollars." I knew he wasn't going to give up on her. He returned the next evening to fix the pipe. Dan told Ester it wouldn't cost her anything except a drink, that he had the pipe lying around the house anyway, just taking up room. I made Dan a drink and the three of us sat in the kitchen at the table sipping on a drink and talking. Ester made me promise not to leave the room until Dan left. I liked Dan. I felt like he was good for Ester. He had a sense of humor. After he left, Ester asked me what I thought of him.

"You're just not used to having a man around. Dan seems nice and has a sense of humor."

Dan called and stopped by the house fairly often. He kept asking her out each time he talked with her. Ester said she would go out with him to eat, but I had to go too. I knew she wasn't totally comfortable dating again so I went with them. The three of us would go up to the truck stop to get a burger or to a great Italian restaurant to have pizza and a Singapore sling. Ester got comfortable enough so I didn't tag along very often anymore. They continued to see each other more and more.

Darren was a friend of mine whom I'd met at the roller skating rink. He was five years younger than I was but he was a lot of fun. He had a great build, strong and sexy. We really got along well. He would come over to Ester's and we tried learning to dance, doing the disco stuff. They had opened a new club in town called the V. I. P. Club for members only. It had three separate bars in the building. They checked your coat when you went in and gave you a ticket to reclaim it when you left. Darren and I would get dressed in disco clothes and go to the club. Neither of us had much money to spend so we usually only had a couple of drinks to sip on for the whole evening. We would have a great time dancing, though.

Dan and Darren would come over to the house and the four of us would sit down by the fire in my room or sit in the kitchen and talk while having a few drinks. Darren was funny when he got around Dan. He would go along with whatever Dan said and laugh when Dan did. The four of us went out to eat at the Italian restaurant quite a bit. The atmosphere was nice in there.

It got to be expensive living at Ester's. The cost of electricity was high in the winter from heating the house. The combination of all utilities was more than rent I would have paid at a place of my own. Darren and I decided to rent a one-bedroom apartment up the street and split rent. Darren said he didn't mind sleeping on the couch, that I could have the bedroom. Someone had given us the couch along with an old coffee table. Ester wasn't happy that I was moving out but she said she understood. I could tell that Darren felt more for me than just friends and our relationship did become more than friends. Darren was irresistible in the physical department. I had told him that nothing serious could come of our relationship. He was younger and had his whole life ahead of him to have a family. I couldn't give him that. He kept trying to get me to marry him. I didn't love him in that same way.

I started going out by myself more. I thought I needed to have Darren realize that we were never going to be more than friends and room mates. I started dating other men but nothing serious. Darren had met a girl and was seeing her some. We continued to share the apartment.

I would get up in the morning and go for a run, go for a swim in the pool, shower and go to work. After work I would go for another run. I was in good physical shape and felt good about myself.

Chapter 7

Wedding Bells Ringing Once Again

Life wasn't too bad. Between our sharing the rent, I had spending money left each week. Ester moved me up from just cleaning rooms to helping in the laundry room. I got more hours of work during the week and Ester gave me a small raise. It was hot in the laundry room and sometimes we worked longer hours on the weekend than I would have liked. I wanted to get home so I could get ready to go out somewhere.

The most popular place to go was the country bar up over the hill from Ester's, Country Junction. Across the street was another bar called The Rebel. It was more of a hang-out for truckers and bikers looking for easy women. I didn't go in there much and rarely when I was alone.

Ester would still go out with me to have a drink on a Saturday night if she wasn't doing anything or seeing Dan. We got off work one Saturday early and I stopped by her house to talk for a few minutes before going to the apartment. The phone rang. Ester asked me to answer it, thinking it may be someone from the motel wanting her to work the next day. She never worked on Sunday unless someone called in sick. "Hello, baby. How ya doing?" the voice said.

"Hello yourself," I replied. It was Dan.

Ester took the phone. "Hi, Dan, what ya know? Oh, you're not? Oh, she is? Okay. I'll talk to you tomorrow." Dan wasn't coming over that evening. His daughter Jill was moving in with Dan for a few weeks and he was going to help her.

"Since Dan isn't coming over, wanna go to the Junction tonight?" I asked Ester.

She thought for a few minutes and then she said, "I'm pretty tired but don't want to sit around here all night by myself either." I told her I would be back in a couple of hours to pick her up.

When I got back to the apartment, Darren was talking to his cousin. He had come over to see Darren. His cousin was a nice boy and always spoke to me politely. He had had a hard upbringing with a lot of responsibilities like Darren had. Darren wanted to know what I had planned to do later.

"Ester and I are going up to the Junction later," I told him.

"Dan going?" he asked with a questioning look on his face. He knew that Dan was usually there at Ester's on Saturday night or they went out together.

"No. His daughter is moving in with him for a few weeks and he's gonna help her move some stuff," I said. Darren waited for a few minutes, like he knew what the answer was going to be to the question he was about to ask.

"Want me to go with ya?"

I knew he was going to ask me that. "Nah, think we'll go by ourselves tonight." I tried not to sound like I really didn't want him to go. It was more like the girls' night out. It was hard to have to keep saying no to Darren when I didn't want him to go. How could I meet or go out with anyone with him tagging along? I didn't like to hurt him, knowing how he felt, and I tried to be as gentle as I could. I'd tell him, "It's not that I don't want us to go out together, but sometimes I like to be alone. We see each other every day."

Darren sort of hung his head. "Guess I'll go see Brenda tonight or go over to my cousin's house and hang out." Brenda was the girl he was seeing some.

It was 7:30 p.m. when I picked up Ester. As soon as I pulled in the driveway, Ester came out of the house. She locked the door behind her and got into the car. Five minutes later we were at the Junction. The place was fairly quiet. A few regulars were sitting up at the bar, drinking and using bad language. They were blitzed so we didn't expect they would be there much longer after the crowd started coming in. We had our choice of seats and we chose to sit away from the door, more in a corner. Ester and I both got our usual Singapore slings from the bar and carried our drinks to the table where we had chosen to sit. The band didn't start playing until nine and we didn't have a lot of money to buy drinks with so we just sipped. About eight-thirty people started coming in and before long the place was full. By then we were ready for another drink. I went to the bar and ordered us another.

The band wasn't too bad. I had been places where the band was so loud and played so badly you had to leave. People were starting to loosen up and dance. The place got really noisy with voices. A young man came over and asked me to dance and I said yes. He couldn't dance very well but it didn't matter, we were there to have fun. He walked me back to our table and introduced himself as Eric. Eric asked if he could buy us both a drink. "Sure," I said. Ester just nodded.

Eric came back with the drinks; he'd gotten a beer for himself. He was looking back and forth at both of us and said, "Mind if I join you two?" Ester looked at me to see the expression on my face and waited for me to answer. I paused for a couple of seconds before I answered the man. I wasn't sure either of us wanted company.

"Yeah, guess so." He sat on a chair between Ester and me, but it wasn't long, after a couple more dances, that he moved closer to me. He seemed nice enough.

It was getting late and I had more than I had planned to drink. I was glad that we both lived so close. Ester said, "It's time to go home, past my bedtime." On that we both got up and reached for our pocketbooks. Eric didn't want me to go but I felt like I had to and I had to take Ester home.

"Will you be up here tomorrow night?" Eric wanted to know.

"Tomorrow is Sunday," I told him. "This place is closed on Sundays."

He continued trying to get to see me the next day. "Hey, you want to go to the park tomorrow, then? I don't have to leave till around seven tomorrow night."

I questioned him, "Why did you want to know if I would be up here tomorrow night if you were leaving?"

"I wasn't thinking," was his quick comeback. In an earlier

conversation, he told us that he was a truck driver, driving for a local company.

"I don't want to go too early," I said. "Tomorrow is Sunday and I want to sleep in awhile." I usually worked on Sunday but it was my Sunday to be off. Eric looked pleased that I agreed.

"How about eleven?" he asked.

"Yeah, eleven is good. Where do you want to meet, or do you want to pick me up at my apartment?"

"I don't have a car, just the truck," said Eric. "Can you come up to the truck stop and get me? I'll be in the restaurant."

I hadn't planned on doing the picking up and using my car but guessed it was all right. I agreed and said I would be there at eleven.

Eric came out of the restaurant as soon as he saw me pull into the parking lot. He seemed eager to get going. I had never been to the park that we went to. It was surrounded by water from the river nearby. Ducks were everywhere. I had brought my camera with me and was able to walk right up to the ducks and take close-up pictures of them. They didn't appear to be afraid of people at all. We walked around the park talking about stuff, not anything really of importance. Eric told me that he made good money driving trucks for this company and told me some about his family. His parents were divorced and both lived in Maryland. His dad had remarried and raised the kids after the separation.

It was getting close to the time for Eric to leave out in the truck. He said he really didn't want to leave but I insisted that he must. I took him back to the truck stop. Before he got out of the car, he asked for my phone number and if it was all right for him to call me when he got back in town. I gave him my number. He leaned over to kiss me and I let him.

I went back to the apartment but Darren wasn't home. He had left me a note saying that he was at his cousin's house and to call him when I got home. I didn't get a chance to call him before he pulled in the parking lot. He came in the apartment. He looked strange. "Thought you'd be home sooner. I tried to call you several times."

"What are you, my father? Keeping tabs on me?" I was a little angry at his behavior.

"No, just concerned," Darren said quietly. *Sweet*

"You needn't be. I'm a big girl; I can take care of myself." I didn't totally believe it myself. I wasn't used to going out by myself or dating except with Darren.

I still cleaned and did laundry for Margie and John on Mondays. Instead of two days of work, I did everything in one. Mondays and Tuesdays were my usual days off at the motel unless I had been off Sunday, then I'd work Tuesday if they needed me. Those were always the slowest days. Margie didn't like the idea of me working only the one day. She felt that I had to hurry too much to clean things properly. If I went to get them dinner, it took me longer in the day, and Margie would tell me, "I'm just so worn out by then." They liked the company. With me coming just one day there was no extra time to sit and talk to them.

Margie and John were happy to see me Monday morning. She already had some extra things for me to do and wondered if I could come back again tomorrow to do them if I was off work from the motel. "I can do whatever you need done today. I'm sure I will have time." Although it didn't take me long to clean the house and do the laundry Margie still didn't want me to do the extra work that day.

"Oh, no. It will take you a while to do this and I don't want you to hurry."

I told her I would call her later to let her know if I could be there the next day.

When I got home from working for Margie, I was tired. I went to the refrigerator and got a cold beer. Darren wasn't home yet. He worked with his dad at the skating rink and did odd jobs. I turned on the TV as the phone was ringing. It was Eric. He just called to say hello and that he should be in tomorrow afternoon. He wanted to see me. "I have to work either at the motel or for Margie tomorrow. Don't know what time I will get off work. What time tomorrow do you think you will get in?" I asked.

"Probably two or three. I'll call you when I get in then," he said. We said good-bye and I hung up the phone. I decided to take a shower before I got too tired. I needed my second wind. I had laundry to do in addition to cleaning the apartment. I started undressing when I heard Darren coming in the door with his cousin. I postponed the shower. I talked to the guys while having another cold beer. Darren's cousin left after about an hour. Darren started questioning me about Eric.

"Are you seeing him again?"

I avoided answering him. I really didn't want to get into it right then. I said, "Probably will," and headed for the shower. Darren was right behind me. "I'm going to take a shower if you don't mind," I said, glaring at him. He walked back in the living room. I knew I hurt his feelings. I didn't like doing that. He was a good friend.

I didn't have to work at the motel the next day so I worked for Margie. The extra work didn't take long to do. I didn't think it would. John didn't ever say much but he liked me to be there so I stayed longer to visit. I was home by lunchtime. I was barely in the door when the phone rang. Eric got in earlier than he thought he would. He said he drove most of the night after he got loaded up the night before. He asked if I would meet him later at the Junction. I hesitated before answering, "I have to work tomorrow so I can't stay out late."

"We can meet early if you want so we will have more time together," said Eric. We set a time of six that evening.

Eric was already there sitting at the bar when I got there. I hopped on the stool next to him and said, "Hi!"

He leaned over and gave me a quick kiss and said, "Hi!" He asked what I wanted to drink.

"A beer will be fine." The beer was cold and tasted good. We moved to a table to be more comfortable and private. We talked for several hours. I was getting tired of drinking beer and sitting there. It was quiet with only a few customers. I suggested that we leave.

"Where you want to go?" Eric asked while walking to the car. I was hungry. I could stand to have something to eat.

"I know of a good Italian restaurant not far from here, if you're hungry."

He got in the car. "Yeah, I'm starving."

We ordered a large pizza. The pizza was good. I felt like I needed to get home and get to bed before it got much later. Eric wanted to know if he could come over to the apartment with me. It was getting late and I needed to get some sleep. I wasn't comfortable having a man come over anyhow, especially until I could get Darren to accept the idea better.

Eric was leaving out again Thursday. He came to the apartment Wednesday evening early. It was a surprise seeing him standing in the open doorway. Darren was there so I was hesitant to let him in at first. I had explained to Eric that I had a roommate and why. If I could have afforded to pay the rent myself I would live there alone. Darren looked up and saw Eric. He got up from where he had been sitting on the floor. I said, "Darren, this is Eric." Darren reluctantly shook Eric's hand. You could feel the tension in the room so I tried to break it by asking Eric, "You want a beer?"

Darren waited for Eric to reply. "Yeah, sure." I think Darren was hoping he would say no and not stay that long.

I gave him a beer and said, "Have a seat." Eric sat on the couch while Darren stood. I remained standing, leaning on the counter top. Eric and Darren started a light conversation, talking about work and general things. He told Darren that he slept in his truck most of the time and took showers at the truck stops. He said there was no reason for him to get an apartment, being alone and on the road so much. He had another beer, then left. He had planned to leave in a few hours so he would be where he was going to unload early when the place opened.

Friday afternoon he was in. He called me at work to let me know. I told him I would come over to the truck stop when I left work to see him. I had to work the next day so I didn't want to go out. I invited him to come to the apartment later. Darren had planned to be there that evening. Everything was going good so far. Ester wanted me to bring Eric up to her house so she could meet him properly. I called Ester to see if she was going to be home later.

"Dan is coming over but we're not going out anywhere." She paused for a couple of seconds. "Give me time to straighten up and take a bath."

"Yeah, I need to take a shower before I pick up Eric, too, so I will see you in a couple hours."

I showered, put on make-up and put on a nice pair of slacks with a matching vest. I went to get Eric. I had to go inside to find him. He was upset about something but he wouldn't say what about, just mumbled something. At Ester's I introduced Eric to Ester and Dan. Darren showed up a few minutes later. He walked in the door. "Didn't want to miss the party."

Ester and Dan laughed, and Dan remarked, "You didn't want to miss something else." Dan and Ester knew that Darren was like a little kid who followed me everywhere. I didn't care that he was there but Eric seemed annoyed. Eric was ready to go after an hour. He wanted to go back to the apartment. He said he wanted to ask me something and couldn't talk to me there.

Eric was leaving Sunday night, going to Chicago to pick up a load. "Since you are off on Monday and if you could be off Tuesday, I would like you to go with me to Chicago. We'd be back by Tuesday afternoon. Want to go?"

I just didn't know. I didn't know Eric that well, and besides, I didn't know if Margie would let me change my day. I would have to go in to work late Tuesday or work around it. "Let me see what I can do about Margie first," I said.

Margie agreed to let me come in the next day on Sunday and work. She wasn't happy with changing her day but knew that I really wanted to go with Eric to get away for a couple of days.

We left about four that afternoon. Eric drove an old truck. It was in rough shape and riding in it was rough. I was thrown all over the cab. I felt like my insides were going to come loose. After a couple of hours of riding, I was getting sleepy. I climbed in the back of the cab and went to sleep. Eric woke me after he had pulled in a truck stop to fuel and to get something to eat. I stayed awake for the remainder of the trip.

In Chicago, we waited at a truck stop for a call to get a load to bring back. Eric couldn't find a load and called his boss to let him know. It sounded as if his boss was upset with Eric. I didn't know what about, and Eric said it was his boss's fault that we were going back empty. That meant less money for the company and less money for Eric.

We got back early that Tuesday. Eric said he was going to go to the truck stop and take a shower and sleep in his truck for awhile. I took a shower at the apartment also. I felt itchy from not having a shower and sleeping in the bunk. I wondered how often that Eric changed his bedding in the bunk. I hoped that I didn't get any bugs or anything from lying in the bunk.

We continued to see each for the next month. Eric said he loved me and wanted us to get married. I loved Eric too. He promised that we would get us a home and a new car. He made all sorts of promises. How could I say no to that? Eric knew that I couldn't have any children but he said he didn't want any more. He had a son by a previous marriage but never got to see him anymore. His ex-wife had gone behind his back and gotten an attorney when she had gotten remarried, and had his son adopted by her new husband.

Ester said we could get married in my old bedroom at her house. We would have a fire in the fireplace and some flowers on the mantle. We found a justice of the peace to marry us. Darren was the best man and an older lady friend of Darren's was my maid of honor. We also had the reception there. There was music playing and Darren and I danced like we used to when we went out together. Eric was drinking a lot. I asked him to slow down. We rented a car and were leaving that evening after the reception, to drive to Maryland. I would meet his family that weekend on our honeymoon. Eric wasn't slowing down at all. "Eric, you have to drive so you better stop drinking," I warned him. We said good-bye to everyone and left. Eric was having difficulty staying on the road. I asked him, "Want to stop at the next motel? We can stay there for the night and leave early in the morning."

His voice was slurred and harsh. "You don't think your husband can drive?" 1st day of marriage

"I think it would be better if we stopped so you can get some sleep. It's been a long day and we are both tired." I tried to humor him. He seemed irritated and I didn't want to make him mad.

"You think Darren could drive better than me? Maybe you should have brought him along. He's always hanging around anyway."

"That isn't true and you know it. I married you. I love you. Why are you acting this way?" I felt uneasy. I had never seen Eric behave like this.

Eric stopped at the next motel. "I'm sorry, you're right. I need to get some sleep." I had to get the room on my credit card because Eric said he didn't have the extra money and he had no credit card. I thought he would have had extra money with all the money he claimed to be making at his job. The room was clean. Eric barely got undressed before he was asleep. I lay in bed thinking that I didn't feel very happy for just getting married. Tomorrow things would be better, I was sure of it.

I woke up early and got in the shower. Eric caught me before I could get dried off completely with the towel and pulled me to the bed. He needed to prove that he was still a man. After all, he did fall asleep before consummating the marriage on our wedding night. I showered again. Eric complained he had a headache and asked if I had some aspirin in my purse. "I don't wonder your head hurts with all you drank last night."

Eric looked pissed. "Don't start! It was my wedding night. Don't I have a right to celebrate?"

I knew I shouldn't have said anything but it just came out of my mouth. After all, it was his wedding night. I didn't reply, knowing this could start an argument. I didn't want to argue. We were newlyweds. I packed up our few personal things in a travel bag and put it in the car. We would only have one night now to spend in Maryland before having to come back. Eric had to go back to work. His boss wouldn't let him take any more time off.

I was hungry. We hadn't had much to eat the day before. I was too nervous over the wedding and getting married. We stopped at a McDonald's to get something to eat while driving. Neither one of us seemed to be in the talking mood. Eric still had a headache; the aspirins hadn't helped much.

It was a long drive to his father and step-mother's house. His dad seemed nice. His step-mom was busy with kids she was caring for. They were the kids of someone in the family who was having problems and couldn't care for them. His brother was a mess. He was into drugs and alcohol at sixteen years old. It felt weird there around his family. His mom lived by herself way out in the country. She was a little strange. I felt uneasy around her. We spent the night sleeping on the couch at Eric's dad's house. I was ready to go back home after hardly getting any sleep that night.

We got back home late that evening. Darren was asleep on the couch. He got up when we came in. "How was your honeymoon?" he asked us, not seeming to really care about the answer.

"Wonderful!" I said, not feeling so wonderful.

Eric gave me a piercing stare. "You didn't like my family or you just don't like me?"

"I didn't say I didn't like your family. It just was a lot of driving and I'm tired out." I didn't know why everything I said got turned around and an argument seemed to be always brewing. "Just wished we had more time than we did for the drive." I hoped that would ease him and he would stop trying to make an argument over something ridiculous.

"I guess because I wanted to celebrate my wedding night, it was my fault we didn't have more time."

"Whatever you say, Eric."

Darren looked almost pleased that we were arguing. I got the feeling that he was enjoying it.

I took the travel bag in the other room and unpacked. Eric was having a beer with Darren. It didn't seem like anyone was ready for bed yet so I had a beer too. Things calmed down between Eric and me. I went to Eric and gave him a kiss. I felt that would make it all right.

It was bedtime. I was exhausted from the ride home. I wanted to lie down and rest. Eric came in the bedroom shortly thereafter.

"I know Darren is a good friend of yours and mine, but I really think he should move out. We don't need him hanging around all the time," Eric whispered to me.

"I don't know where he would go. Back to his parents' house, I guess. I would feel bad to have to tell him that he has to move out. He has been a good friend to me." I really didn't want to discuss it at that time. I was afraid that I would say something to make Eric mad again. I was too tired to think straight anyhow. "Eric, I will talk to Darren tomorrow and see how he reacts. That way he can have time to find a place." Eric went along with it and we went to sleep.

Darren wasn't working the next day and neither was I. Eric had to leave early that morning in the truck. I made myself and Darren some coffee and brought up the dreaded subject that I knew I would have to talk to him about. "Darren?" I said.

"Yeah, what?"

"I was wondering where you would move to if you weren't staying here."

Darren had a puzzled look on his face. "What do you mean?"

"I mean if Eric and I wanted to live here by ourselves, where would you go?"

"Dad's, I guess. Why, does Eric want me to move out?" Eric did and in a way I did too. I knew if Darren continued to stay there and with Eric gone so much on the road, there was sure to be some distrust and jealousy.

"With Eric gone so much, it doesn't look right for a man to be staying here with a married woman."

Darren said he would try to find someplace else to stay.

I was still seeing my psychologist from when Russell and I were having problems. I was not sleeping very well these days. I had an appointment to see him that day. Maybe he would give me something to help me sleep and not be so down in the dumps. I wasn't happy with the way things were going with Eric and me and wondered if I had made a mistake marrying him. I couldn't believe what a bastard he had become since we got married. He had changed like day changes to night. My psychologist gave me a prescription for an antidepressant. I was to take one a day. I started taking the pills immediately. I continued to take them but they weren't helping, and it seemed as if I was more depressed than before. It would probably just take more time to get in my system, so I had to be patient.

Nothing had been said about Darren moving out by either one of us in the next few days. He was good company to me while Eric was gone. Eric had called and asked me if I had talked to Darren about moving. "Yes, I did the next day after we talked about it. I think he is looking but hasn't said anything yet."

"I'll be in tonight," Eric informed me.

"Oh, really? I thought you wouldn't be in until tomorrow night." I didn't understand.

"They gave the load I was supposed to have to one of the other drivers so I am coming home empty." He didn't sound too upset over it. I would have been.

"Well, you can't make any money like that!" I wasn't sure I believed him. There had been too many things that weren't adding up lately.

Before Eric came home, Darren left. He said he would just as soon to not be there when Eric got home. He said he would stay at his cousin's that evening and talk to me the next day. I made us something to eat. It wasn't much because there wasn't much in the apartment to eat. Darren and I were the only ones to buy food. Eric never did but he expected to have something to eat. I complained that he needed to give me some money if he wanted to eat. "Let Darren buy the food. He eats here all the time," Eric snapped at me.

"Darren doesn't eat here much at all and when he does he buys it."

"You always take up for him. You care more for him than you do me." I could tell he was getting to the point that I didn't want to talk to him anymore.

"Just forget it, Eric. You don't make any sense at all," I snapped back at him.

Eric didn't have another load until the weekend, but I still had to work. Darren called the next night and asked if he could come over. He said he was bored at his cousin's and wanted to come over and talk to us. "Sure you can. We're not doing anything tonight, just watching TV." Eric didn't seem to mind. He didn't seem very happy that I hadn't asked him first, but he got over it.

Chapter 8

The Horror!

Darren arrived at the apartment about seven-thirty. Eric and he talked but it hadn't been brought up yet about Darren moving out. Darren said he was hungry. "I got some extra money that I made on a job yesterday. Want to go out and have pizza? I'll buy." Eric jumped at that idea. He would take a person's last dollar, he didn't care. I wanted to go but didn't want Darren to buy. Darren didn't make much money. Everything he did make went to pay bills, not that he had that many.

"Yeah, we'll go," Eric answered for both of us.

I showered and changed my clothes. We took our car. Darren only had his cousin's old truck and I didn't want to ride in that. The pizza and beer were good. We hadn't been out in a long time and the walls were starting to close in on me. I was used to going out some before Eric and I got married. Darren stayed at the apartment that night so he wouldn't have that long drive to his cousin's.

Eric was gone for a couple of days again. Darren came over and we talked about Eric and me and how bad things had gotten between us. "He has changed so much," I said to Darren. "He thinks I am supposed to jump when he says so and yells at me when I ask him anything about his paycheck. He claims that the company is cheating him out of his pay, that's why he never has any money. I have never seen a paycheck yet. He says he has to cash it at the truck stop to get fuel and money to run on. I hate to think he is lying to me, but I think he is. He gets so mad when I question him about it." I thought of how

I could find out what was really going on. I didn't dare call the company where he worked and didn't think they would tell me anything anyhow.

When Eric got in the next time, I asked him if he would not cash his check so I could look at it and see if we could figure out what was going on. ["You think I'm lying about my check? You little bitch. I knew you would turn on me just like everyone always has."] He was furious. I tried to calm him down and tell him that I just didn't think he should get cheated, that he worked too hard for his money. He went to the refrigerator and got a beer. He drank it down fast. He got another, the whole time not talking to me. "I think I'll look for another job. I saw where this one company is hiring and I know they pay good and have good benefits too. If this company doesn't straighten out, I'll quit." He had calmed down some by then.

verbal abuse

"If you think that is a good idea." I went along but didn't agree that it was a good idea. I didn't believe that the company was cheating him but didn't know where the money was going.

Eric had brought the truck home the next time he was in. If he was leaving soon after he had gotten in, he said it was a waste of time to park it at the company's lot. He had planned to leave a few hours after he had slept. I waited until he was deep asleep and got my purse to walk next door to the convenience store. I went by the side of the truck so that I wouldn't be seen if he should be looking out the apartment window. I carefully opened the driver's side door, kept my head down and crawled in. I was on my belly on the seat with my feet hanging out the door. The street lights gave enough light so I could see if there were any papers on the floor. I found several and one of them was a pay stub. I crammed it in my pocket and jumped down from the truck and closed the door. I looked to make sure Eric wasn't around to see me and ran over to the store. When I got back to the apartment, Eric was sitting on the couch. "Where you been?" I hated that tone of voice. I felt like smacking him when he sounded that way.

"I went to the store to get a candy bar. I wanted something sweet for a change." He looked like he thought I was up to something but didn't say anything further.

I watched the clock when Eric wasn't looking, hoping he would

110

hurry up and leave so I could look at the stub. I opened the stub as soon as I heard the truck go up the road but stood by the window to keep watch in case he forgot something and came back. Wow, he made twice as much as he had claimed. They had deducted money that Eric had taken out of his check during the week before payday. What was he spending that money on? I knew I would have to confront him when he came in. I couldn't help thinking of stories that I had heard about truck drivers. Sometimes when they were on the road, they would pick up women to sleep with. Eric wouldn't pay for women, would he? I wondered how much he went to the bars when he was on the road, and if he bought drinks not only for himself but for women as well. I hated thinking any of this could be true but I didn't know the answers.

I talked to Darren about finding the stub. He, of course, agreed with me that he thought Eric was lying to me. I was glad that I was still taking medication for depression even though I didn't really feel any different. I couldn't help thinking about what I would say to Eric or how would I explain having the pay stub. It worried me that he would really get mad. I was becoming afraid of him and it didn't take much to piss him off. Most of the time he would come home pissed off about something that happened that day and take it out on me.

A couple days later when Eric came home, I approached him about the pay stub. "I found this pay stub. I don't understand why you took money out of your check before payday." I was trying to be careful with the way I asked him to explain. "You have money with you when you leave. What do you need more money for?" I could tell by his red face that he was furious.

"You don't know anything. You think that little money that I have is enough? I got fuel, tolls and what do you want me to do, starve? Yeah, you probably do. You don't love me. You don't even try to understand me." He was so upset that he kept talking about things that had nothing to do with what was at hand. I couldn't get a word in. He wasn't even making any sense. I waited until he slowed down with his yelling so I could get a few words in.

"You told me that the company pays you back for tolls and fuel. I see on the pay stub where they did but you took out more than that.

I don't believe that the company is cheating you; you are just lying to me and doing something else with the money. Do you think I am going to put up with a liar? What else do you lie to me about?" Eric came over to me and grabbed my arms. He was holding me by my wrist so tight I could feel the circulation stopping. Eric was in a rage.

"What, you saying you don't want to be with me anymore? Well, I got news for you, you ain't going nowhere." I tried to get loose but his grip was too tight. The more I struggled the tighter his grip was and the worse the pain.

I finally said, "No, I was just mad when I said that." Eric let go of me. We didn't discuss the pay stub any further.

The next time Eric left on a run, I thought about where I could go to stay if I left Eric. I thought if Eric wanted to stay in the apartment he could and I would get another. I could find a cheap apartment that I could afford. I was afraid of how Eric would react if I really did leave him. I knew at this point that he was violent.

Eric came home and seemed to be in a good mood. "Want to go out to eat tonight?" he asked me.

"Yeah, I guess." I didn't dare say no, even though I really didn't want to go anyplace with him. We went to eat at the pizza place. We had pizza and a couple of beers. I didn't want to talk to him because I didn't want another episode like the last one, but I felt I needed to. I told him that I wasn't happy, that nothing he promised or said before we got married was true. I knew I was taking a chance by saying those things. Eric didn't say much. He just mumbled something and asked if I was ready to go. Back at the apartment all hell broke loose. Eric grabbed me by the arms again and shook me like I was a child.

"You're not going to leave me, I'll kill you."

He was really hurting my arms. I knew he may really hurt me more so I tried to calm him by saying, "We will work it out. I'm not leaving."

"You're mine and no one else is going to have you. You hear me? You're mine." Eric looked like a crazy person. His face was all distorted and red with fury.

"Okay, Eric, just let me go. Please let go of me." My arms were bruised and hurt. I knew that I was definitely going to leave him. I would get the law to help keep him away from me.

While Eric was gone on the road the next time, I got really sick with the flu. I had gone to work even though I really felt bad. After work, at the apartment, I tried to clean up the place and wanted to get some laundry done. Eric came home. I was in no mood to put up with him but didn't have much choice. He was there. He saw that I was really sick and that I was trying to fold laundry. He took the basket from me and said he would do it for me. "I can do it, I'm not helpless," I told him. He started ranting and raving about things; I had no idea what he was talking about again. I told him I was too sick to listen to him and I was going to get some rest.

He grabbed me and said, "You're gonna listen to me, what I have to say." I sat down on the couch while he went in the bathroom. I got up with my purse in hand and went out the door. The car was right outside the door so I was quick to get in and drive off before he realized I had gone.

I didn't know where to go so went over to my ex-sister-in-law Rhonda's house. Russell was there but Rhonda and Bob had gone on vacation. Russell was taking care of the dog and bringing in the mail. "You look awful," Russell said as soon as he saw me.

"Thanks, I feel awful. Got the flu." I knew he was probably wondering what I was doing there. "I couldn't get any rest at the apartment. Eric is such an asshole and I was afraid he would hurt me again." I hadn't meant to blurt all that out to him but it just came out.

Russell put his arm around my waist and helped me to the couch. He made me some soup and I ate it while we talked. I told him what was going on. "Rhonda won't be back for a week. Put your car in the garage and you can stay here until you feel better. Eric won't think to look for you here." The phone rang and it was Eric. Russell told him that I wasn't there and that he hadn't seen me. The phone continued to ring all night but I didn't answer it. Russell came over first thing in the morning to check on me. He said Eric was calling there all night too.

I stayed there two nights and felt better. The second morning I was on my way into the bathroom when I saw Eric looking in the kitchen window and could hear him cussing me. I didn't let him in; instead, I went to the bathroom and stayed there until I felt he may

113

be gone. The phone rang and rang and rang. I left Rhonda's house and went back to the apartment. I didn't know where else to go. Eric wasn't there yet. The phone rang. It was Eric.

"Finally decided to come home? I have been looking all over for you."

"You wouldn't let me get any rest here so I had to go somewhere," I defended myself. He told me not to leave and that he would be there in a minute. He said he missed me and thought I had left him for good. He said we would talk and he wouldn't touch me.

Eric slammed the door behind him with such force it jarred the pictures on the wall. He came over to where I was standing in the kitchen and hit me in the head. "You bitch! Sleeping with Russell? Didn't think I would find out? Go back to him if you want him. I don't want you anyhow." I was crying and hoped that he would calm down before he hurt me more but he hit me again. I tried to get out of the apartment but he grabbed my shirt and then my arm. "You're not going anywhere. You think I'm going to let you go that easy? You belong to me." I knew I had to go along and pretend that I didn't want to leave him and that I loved only him. That would be my only chance to keep him from hurting me more.

Things settled down and he wanted to make love and make up. I couldn't stand the thought of him touching me; it made me sick to my stomach. I couldn't take any more beating so I let him have his way. Afterwards he fell asleep. I felt like running away but where would I go?

I was happy to see Eric leave again. I felt like maybe this was my fault. Maybe I could be a better wife to him. Maybe if I tried harder he would be better to me. Maybe it was my fault when Russell and I split up. I wished I could just die. I wasn't a good person; that was why this was happening to me. I didn't see any way out. He wouldn't ever let me go. I would do the best I could not to make him mad or question him about anything. I felt empty inside—no feelings, like a motionless figurine.

It was Saturday afternoon and I had just gotten home. Darren called and asked if Eric and I wanted some company. Nothing had still been said about Darren moving out but he just didn't make it a

114

habit of being at the apartment all the time. His rent was still paid until the end of the month. "Eric isn't home yet but should be home shortly. He's usually home early if it is on the weekend. Yeah, sure, come on over. He should be here by the time you get here." I hoped that Eric got there before Darren. I didn't want another fight.

"I got a bottle of Black Velvet. Want me to bring it? Haven't had a good drink since we went out dancing." Darren sounded excited about coming over. I hadn't seen him in awhile. It would be good to see a friendly face for a change. That sounded good. I could use a good drink.

"Yeah, man. Sounds good," I told Darren.

Darren arrived before Eric did. We mixed a drink of Black Velvet and Coke, but not too strong. I didn't like to really taste the liquor in the drink. Eric's face lit up when he saw Darren. I couldn't tell if he was happy to see him or if he just had a good day for a change. "Where's mine?" Eric grinned. Darren was surprised at Eric grinning and went immediately to fix him a drink.

"Here you go."

"How long you two been drinking?" Eric questioned us.

"Darren just got here. He called me and said he had some Black Velvet and thought we might want a few drinks. I thought you would have been here by the time Darren got here but I know you never know for sure what time you'll be in." I was being cautious in choosing my words in hopes he wouldn't get mad.

I was standing in the kitchen leaning on the counter top and listening to Eric and Darren talk. Darren was standing closer to the kitchen than the living room. I turned to go to the bathroom. Darren said something to me but I didn't hear him. I stopped and turned around and about ran into Darren he was so close. Eric jumped up and leapt toward Darren, pushing him into the wall next to the bathroom. Eric hit Darren in the face with his fist, making him bleed. I screamed at Eric to stop but he continued to hit Darren. They were hitting each other and calling each other names.

God, what have I done? I asked myself. This was my fault. I should have never let Darren come over. Eric and Darren had managed to get outside and I could hear them fighting. I couldn't let this happen anymore. If I wasn't here, there would be no reason for fighting. I didn't want to deal with it anymore.

I took a big swallow of liquor, and then another. My medication was sitting on the counter. I washed down all the pills with Black Velvet. I went outside. I wasn't afraid of him anymore. I could say what I wanted. He couldn't hurt me. Both of them were bloody but weren't fighting as wildly as before. I wanted to say what was on my mind. "You son-of-a-bitch! I hate you. You won't ever hurt me again. I won't be here for you to hurt, you bastard. I hate you. I hope you go to hell." Eric started to come after me but Darren stopped him. "This is all my fault, but I won't cause anymore problems for no one." I was feeling woozy by then. I wasn't sure how my words were coming out or if anyone could hear me.

"You're drunk!" Eric said.

"Yep, a little," I slurred out. I could see Darren just standing like he was thinking hard about something.

"What did you do? You didn't take anything, did you? What did you mean you won't be here for Eric to hurt you? What did you mean?" Darren was real nervous and kept moving around in circles. He was making me dizzier than I already was. He kept talking like he was trying to figure out what was happening. "Eric, I think she may have taken those pills she had. Did you?" he demanded.

It was getting harder to talk and I was getting sleepy. "I don't have to answer any questions if I don't want. Don't ever have to answer questions."

We were in the apartment now. Darren was on the phone. I couldn't hear much of the conversation. I didn't know who he was talking to. "I'm going to sleep." I could barely put one foot in front of the other but I was trying to get to the bed. Everything was getting hazy. Eric was all upset about something. I wished he would be quiet. I wanted to sleep but instead I was walking, walking, forever walking. "I got to rest. I'm so tired."

"You can't sleep, you have to walk." Darren was crying.

It was cold in the shower. *Turn on some warm water*, I thought. *Who is this man holding me in the shower?* I didn't want to stay awake. *Let me sleep.*

My head hurt. *Where am I?* I had tubes all over my body. It hurt to open my eyes. My stomach and chest were full of pain and I couldn't swallow. I felt like I had been severely beaten. I couldn't be alive. *No, I don't want to be here.* I managed to turn my head to see Eric sitting beside the bed in a chair. *Please don't let me be alive. I'm not supposed to be here. I can't bear to look at his face. I hate him,* I thought in my aching head. Words, lies.

Eric saw that I was awake and came over to the side of the bed. "I thought you were dead for sure, but you made it. I'm going to be a good husband to you from now on. I don't want to lose you." He was waiting for a response. I was not able to say anything and he looked as if he was about to get mad. "You do want to stay with me, don't you?" I knew I had to try to say something so he would shut up.

"Yeah, of course," was all I could get out. Eric wouldn't shut up. My head hurt so bad that the least little noise felt like a bomb going off in my head.

"When they brought you in, you weren't breathing. They had to really work on you to get you to start breathing and then they didn't know if you would make it or not."

Eric continued to ramble until I stopped him by asking, "How long have I been here? What day is this?"

"It's Tuesday," he said. "I was going with a load to Chicago tonight but called the office and told them that my wife was in the hospital so I couldn't go."

"If you need to go, go! I will be all right." I hoped he would go but wants he wouldn't. *I can't do anything right, not even kill myself,* I kept to thinking as I lay there wishing I were dead. die

My doctor set me up for counseling. I had to go once a week for a month and then the doctor would evaluate me and see how I had progressed. I hated going. I knew it was a waste of time. It wouldn't do any good until I could get rid of the real problem, Eric. I went along with whatever Eric wanted and Darren said I was crazy to put up with him. Darren called once in a while to see how I was doing, and when I could I would go see him at his cousin's. Darren made me laugh and I needed that. He had always been there for me.

I was starting to feel better. It was time to make some changes. I would save my money to get another apartment. Once Eric realized I was serious and didn't want to be with him, I knew he would leave me alone. I found an efficiency apartment on the edge of city limits in Youngstown. It was about ten minutes away from the old apartment. I waited for Eric to leave on a run to Indiana, and as soon as I felt it was safe, I started moving my things in the car. Darren got his cousin to come over in his truck and we moved the little bit of furniture that I had. I was so frightened that when he got back he would find me. At least he wouldn't be able to get in.

I went to work the next day. Ester knew that I had moved and knew of all that was going on with Eric and me. I was afraid of coming out of rooms after cleaning them to go to the next one. My heart was always in my throat and my nerves were shot. Ester would go check in the hallway for me when I finished a room to make sure Eric wasn't around. At the front office they was screening any calls I got and watching for him in the parking lot. When I left to go home, someone would walk me to my car and wait until I was in the car with the doors locked.

I had just gotten my phone hooked up. It was good to have the phone in case Eric came around and I needed to call for help. The phone rang. It was Eric.

"Thought you could get away from me. Wasn't hard to find you. I don't understand why you left. Things were going good with us." He really didn't understand at all.

"I told you I didn't want to be with you. I think we need to be apart for a while and maybe that would help. We can talk if you want." I knew there was no way I would ever go back to him but I had to make him think that so he would leave me alone. Eric's voice was low.

"No sense in me keeping the apartment here without you. I'll just sleep in the truck and when I'm in maybe you might let me stay with you."

"No, that won't work. I told you I need to be away from you for a while." I was getting angry and worried that he would start coming over. "Can't you just leave it alone for now? It's only going to make things worse if you don't."

"But I love you and don't want to lose you." He was crying now. I was happy he was crying. I hoped he hurt just like I did.

"If you don't leave me alone for a while, you'll never see me again," I said sternly. We hung up. Maybe I could have a little peace, at least for tonight.

Eric showed up at work the next day. Ester told him he should leave and that I wasn't going to see him. He left only to go to a phone booth to call the office and asked for me. They refused to let him talk to me, saying we couldn't accept any personal calls. The phone was ringing as soon as I got home and walked in the door. I knew it was probably Eric so I didn't answer the phone. It continued to ring until I couldn't stand it anymore. I took the phone off the hook. I put my gun, which I had gotten when Russell and I split up, under the pillow that I kept on the couch. I slept on the couch instead of in bed. The couch was next to the door, and if anyone came in I could hear them. I had heavy curtains up over the sliding glass door in the living room. You couldn't see in or out but you could see a shadow with the lights off. I didn't sleep much at night. I would hear things and wonder if it was Eric.

I hadn't heard from or seen Eric for a couple of days. A girlfriend I had recently met invited me out to eat. We met at the truck stop and took her car out to eat. I left mine there in the parking lot. I had a good time for a change, relaxing some knowing Eric was probably out of town. She dropped me off at my car and waited while I looked in to make sure no one was there. I waved to her that it was all right and she left. I started the car and noticed that the inside lights were not working. My headlights were on, but no low beam. My directional lights were not working either. I knew that Eric must be back in town. He probably thought that I was out with another man with my car sitting there. I couldn't believe he'd done this to my car.

I was just putting the key in the door of the apartment when I felt someone take my arm. I jumped back. I thought my heart would come out of my chest, it was pounding so hard. "Let me in. I just want to talk to you. Please. I love you." He was about to start crying. Although he looked pathetic, I said no.

"I don't want you in here. You can call me and I will talk to you but I don't want you to come in." I was firm but afraid. Eric let go and said

119

FIGHT

talking)

Quote

RAPE

all right and turned to leave. As I opened the door, I felt a push. Eric pushed his way in and he had his arm around my throat. He had his other hand holding mine behind him. I reached for the cast iron fry pan that I kept on the stove, and with my free hand I hit Eric as hard as I could. He let go of me and I ran for the door but he caught me again. He threw me across the living room floor with such force that I fell against the side of the wall. Eric kicked me on my back and kicked me in the head. I saw his fist coming at me so I ducked and he hit the wall. He forced me on the floor and was tearing at my clothes. "You're my wife. You'll give me sex whenever I want it." I begged him not to do this and tried to fight him but he was too strong.

Eric rolled off me. I got up and went into the bathroom and threw up. I felt dirty and hurt. I pulled up my jeans and peeked out the bathroom door to see where Eric was. He had gotten up and was looking out the sliding glass door smoking a cigarette. I had to make a run for it. I was outside the front door but Eric wasn't far behind. I was running wildly in the parking lot and screaming, "Call the cops! Someone call the cops! He's gonna kill me!" Eric had me by my hair and I was trying to get out of his grasp. Several people looked out the window of their apartments but no one seemed to want to help me. A woman in the apartment across the lot yelled out to me, "The cops are on their way." That scared Eric and he took off around the building. The lady asked me if I wanted to come up on her deck until the law got there. I was afraid to stay standing in the parking lot.

The cops asked if I wanted to file a complaint. I told them yes. They said to call the district attorney in the morning but for now to go in the apartment and get some things and stay with a friend. I had met Cathy through her husband, who was also a truck driver. Eric had met Tommy at the truck stop. I liked Cathy and thought she would let me stay there. I got in my car and was driving down the road when I saw Eric jump out in front of the car. I don't think I slowed down. I don't remember. He jumped back to the side of the road when he realized I wasn't stopping. The police found him and took him to the station. It wasn't long after that he was released.

I stayed at Cathy's that night and the next day. I got a restraining order and talked to the district attorney. He said we would sue Eric and he would never have anything. I tried to explain to the D.A. that it wouldn't do any good to sue a person who doesn't have anything and will never have anything. I didn't understand why they didn't keep him in jail in the first place.

I stayed with Cathy several more days. I needed to get back to the apartment to get some things. Cathy said she would go with me but we decided it would be safer if we walked. It wasn't far away. It was drizzling and chilly. We waited until it got dark and walked as close to shadows as possible, so as not to be seen. We went in the back door of the apartment building after checking around for any sign of Eric. I unlocked the apartment door and slipped off my shoes. "I'll go get some things," I told Cathy.

"What're you getting?" I heard Eric's voice and froze. He was standing in the kitchen behind the wall so he hadn't been visible on entering the apartment. There were dirty dishes all over the countertop, in the sink and on the stove. It looked as if he had been there for some time. I turned to go out the door but there wasn't time enough before he stopped me. "What you need is a good spanking. Yeah, that's what you're gonna get. I'm tired of messing with you." At that he pulled me down on my stomach over his legs. He spanked me like I was a child. Cathy tried to get to the phone but he pulled it from the wall. Cathy went into the bedroom. She opened a window and crawled out. When Eric was finished with his spanking, he let me go. I could hear Cathy calling me to the bedroom. I was crying and didn't know how we would get back out of there.

"Come on, hurry," Cathy whispered. I hurried to the window and was almost out when Eric spotted me. We ran for the woods behind the building. I was barefoot and the cold, wet branches were piercing my feet. Out on the main road, we stayed behind the shadows of the buildings. Cathy was trembling as much as I was, not only from the cold but from being so frightened. "He's crazy! He's a whacko! He needs help!" Cathy was furious and went on to say, "How degrading, spanking a grown person and in front of someone. He is disgusting." It was degrading. I'd had rather he'd hit me than spanked me.

The cops went over to my apartment after I called them. They called me back and said there was no sign of a break-in so no charges could be filed. He was being arrested after they had seen him outside the sliding glass door. One of the officers fell in a hole and broke his leg while trying to apprehend Eric. They were quite upset. As before, Eric was released again shortly after taking him in. Couldn't they find some reason to keep him there?

I was asked to turn in the gun I had to the police station. "It's registered and it's mine. I need it to protect myself." I wasn't about to give it up without a fight.

"We'll give it back; we just want to check it out." One of the officers said that Eric had told them that I had a gun and had threatened to shoot him. I probably did. They were afraid that I might really shoot him so I never got the gun back.

Management said I had to move. They wouldn't put up with police having to come all the time. They were afraid that Eric would do something to cause damage to the apartment. I had to drive my car with it the way that it was. I couldn't afford to get it fixed right now. I got stopped by the cops and was fined twenty dollars for driving with no turn signals.

I junked the car and went to a local used car dealer. I got a car on credit and the owner set me up with small payments so I could afford to pay for it.

I moved to a new place down the road. Eric begged me to let him stay there, that things would be different. "I will on one condition. We get a divorce." I explained to him that if we got a divorce and started over, it would make a big difference.

"Okay, I will, but I know you will marry me again. You'll see things will be different." I knew if I let him stay with me he wouldn't beat on me for a few months. YOU'RE STUPID

I saw Eric that evening but he was heading out again with a load someplace in Indiana. I decided to go out to one of the local bars, which was only a couple of miles away, the next evening. The weatherman had been calling for some showers but that didn't bother me. The bar wasn't crowded. I kept having the feeling that Eric would walk in so I was careful about who I talked to. A man came in and said it was raining hard outside so if anyone had windows down in their car it would be a good idea to put them up. I ran out of the bar to put my windows up. I had another draft beer and talked with a man sitting four seats from me. He asked to move closer so he could hear me better but I said no, that I was expecting company. The television was on but no one seemed to be paying any attention until the bulletin about the tornado. A tornado had hit only ten miles away, close to where Margie and John lived. I left the bar to go home to try to call Margie and see if they were okay. The lines were down.

The next morning I got in my car and drove toward their house. It looked like a war zone. Electric lines and phone lines were lying all over the place along with other debris. Roads were blocked off and I couldn't get to the road Margie lived on. I asked one of the men working there if the houses on Margie's road were okay. He said yes, that their street was one the tornado didn't get. Thank goodness.

I got the divorce from Eric without any complications. I felt like I'd have a better chance to get him out of my life not being married to him.

In the next several months we made a decision to move to New Hampshire. I had always liked it there. I would be closer to my family and to the beach. Eric loaded up my furniture in the truck that he had been driving for the company. I would drive my car. He said he was quitting his job and would use the truck to move and leave it there in Massachusetts in a rest area. He would call the company and tell them the location of the truck. I had hoped that he would get caught and be arrested but he got away with it.

The drive to New Hampshire was long and tiresome but it gave me time to think. I had to make a plan once we got there of what I could do and where I could go to get him out of my life.

Eric's brother and wife lived in Massachusetts. Eric had called them before we left Ohio. I had talked to them once before. They sounded like nice people. It was almost dark when we arrived at their house. His sister-in-law, Kimberly, was very nice. I hadn't heard that New England accent for a while. It made me feel good, like I was home again. They had a big old house that they were remodeling. It belonged to her grandmother and had been given to them. Josh, his brother, and he didn't seem to be very close but I didn't ask any questions.

Eric and I went to look for a place to rent the next day. We found a place up in Rochester, New Hampshire. It was farther out in the country than I would have liked. The rent was more than we could really afford but we couldn't find much else that was decent. We both had to find jobs soon. All the money we had was gone on the rent and deposit. We had no money to buy food but we had enough to buy gas to look for jobs. Eric got a job at a grading company in Portsmouth. He used the car to go back and forth to work. I stayed at the apartment for two weeks until Eric got his first check so we would have gas money enough for me to take him to work and look for a job myself.

I got a job working at a motel as a housekeeper. The pay wasn't good and it was only part-time. The fighting was still going on but not as bad. Two months passed and we knew we would have to move out soon. We couldn't afford the rent, and it was too far to drive to work. We found an apartment at Hampton Beach. The rent was reasonable. It had a sliding glass door off the kitchen that went on to a deck. One of the bedrooms had a twin bed in it. It had just enough room to walk in and turn around. I put my stereo in that room so I could have some quiet time when I wanted to relax. I listened to classical music. I had music by Mozart, Bach, Beethoven, and music that had sounds from the ocean. I went down to the beach every day that I could. I missed the ocean. I would feed the seagulls and talk to them as they came down close to me. They were my friends.

I looked up my old friend April, whom I had worked with before when I lived there. She had gotten married to the guy she had been dating years ago. I told her I was looking for a job and asked if she knew of anyone hiring.

"They're hiring where I work. I can get you an application tomorrow if you want. The pay is good but you've got to work long hours," she told me. I filled out the application as soon as I picked it up from her. I took it to the plant the next day. I got hired the next week. It was mandatory fifty hours a week and usually we worked four or five hours on Saturdays. The pay was good and with the overtime, I knew I could put some money away to save. I got a safe deposit box at the bank and put jewelry, money and anything else in it I was afraid that Eric might take.

Eric
Fired

Eric got fired from his job and took another truck driving job. He was only home a few days a week. Whenever he was home it was a series of arguments. He would come home smelling of alcohol. The fighting would start. It was worse when he drank; he was so physically and mentally abusive. He would say things like, "Who have you been screwing while I've been busting my ass working for you? I wouldn't have to work like a dog if it wasn't for you." Then he would hit me. He was so warped. He disgusted me.

Eric lost his job again. He said he quit at first but I called the company and they said they fired him for drinking on the job. Said they couldn't afford to lose the business in a lawsuit. Eric came in the door screaming at me. "It's all your fault I got fired. If I wasn't so stressed out all the time, I wouldn't have to drink. You're just a bitch; no one would want you. Go, get out. I don't want you either." That sounded like a good idea. I got my purse and started for the door. "You're not taking that with you. You won't take nothing from here. The car will stay here. If you want to go then you can walk." I fought to keep my purse. There was no way he was having my purse and my car keys. Eric threw me on the floor. I got up and started walking very slowly toward the door. I ran out and got to the car. He caught me and pushed me in the car and then he slid in the driver's side. "You wanna go for a ride?" he said. "I'll take you for a ride." He was so drunk and was driving like a crazy man, all over the road and way too fast. I tried to jump out; death would have been better than having to live through this. The way he was driving I could have gotten killed. I could only hope that if we wrecked, he would be killed instead. Eric drove back to the apartment, parked the car, and got out. He opened up the hood and pulled two of the spark plug wires off. "Drive it now," he said and went back in the apartment. I stayed outside for a long time in hopes that maybe he would be passed out when I went in. He was.

I found a nice apartment across the road from where I was working. It was a one bedroom. It was about time to move out from the beach. It was a winter rental. They would rent the apartment out in the summer and ask three times as much as in the winter. I told Eric that he wasn't moving with me. That was the end of the line. "You

Quote

will never change. I've been beaten and abused all that I'm going to be. If you ever try to hurt me again, I will kill you." I moved in my new apartment. Eric called and came over. I played the game and reminded him of how good we were getting along now. I made him think that if he stayed away and got his own place, we might have a chance of getting back together.

"Do you think you would marry me again? I love you and just want things to work out. I'll get a place and then we can visit each other, like we were dating," he said eagerly. I had to stay calm and not get angry. I didn't know anything anymore but hate, anger and being frightened.

"You never know, this could change everything," I convinced him.

It had been a year now. I had managed to save enough money that when the time came I could leave and not worry for a while. Eric kept pestering me to marry him and when I would come up with some excuse that it wasn't time yet, he would get angry. I learned to play the game with him instead of trying to fight him. I hated the sex the worst but I had to see this to the end.

One night I refused to see him when he called. I said I was so worn out from work that I needed to go to sleep. He showed up the next day at work looking for me. I told him that I would see him later at the apartment. I thought that he would have been at my apartment on my arrival but he wasn't. In the apartment I found pictures from my album torn up in pieces. An empty bottle of wine was broken on the floor. My bed was in shambles and blank checkbooks were scattered all over the place. There was dirt on the floor from where the plants had been turned over. I checked in my checkbook and saw that three checks were missing. The phone rang; it was Eric. "You bastard, I hate you. I hate you. Why did you do this? You better bring back those checks." I was more furious than I had ever remembered being.

"I was just mad at you because you wouldn't see me last night. I threw the checks away." I didn't believe him. "Can I come over?"

"No! You ruin everything. Just when I thought I might consider marrying you again." *Liar, liar,* I thought. *I will never marry you again.*

"I promise I won't do anything like this again. Give me another chance. I just love you so much and want you to be my wife again." He was about to cry.

"You give me back the blank checks, then," I demanded.

"I told you I threw them away. I just took them to make you think I would write one and cash it. That's against the law. I'm not getting in trouble with the law."

I still didn't believe him.

The deadbolt on my door was broken. The manager said it would cost me to replace it and wanted to know when I was going to make up the bounced check that I had given her for rent. My mouth dropped open. "What? That check is good. I don't understand." She didn't seem to want to hear what I had to say. I explained that when Eric broke in, he took some blank checks. She said she felt bad that this happened and that I had been a good tenant up until now. She said I needed to move out with all the problems with Eric. I broke down in tears, more determined to get rid of him. I got what was left of my deposit after the new lock was put on.

— Now stealing from her
Had to move twice b/c of Eric.

Chapter 9

Plans in the Making

My supervisor said that I could stay with her and store my bed and dresser in her dad's old barn. "He won't find you here. You can ride to work with me." I got a job working with a cleaning company five nights a week on top of my regular job. I saved all the money I made from that job. Mary wasn't charging me any rent to stay there.

My car broke down and I was told it wasn't worth fixing. I had to find another one soon. I had to give up the cleaning job, not having any transportation. Eric came to my workplace constantly. The human resource person where I worked suggested I take a leave of absence and go stay at a battered women's shelter for a while. I agreed to go. Mary set it up for me. She took me to a drop-off place where a lady from the shelter would take me to the home from there.

We had counseling meetings that were mandatory for everyone to attend. The cleaning chores were done equally by all the women staying there. Everyone bought their own food and did their own cooking. A young woman with two small children was staying there. Her husband had shot her in the head but she only had a small scar from the bullet. The bullet just grazed the side of her head, luckily for her. She had gone back to him many times before after leaving him, but swore this time was the last. He had beaten her each time she returned back home. We talked about our situation all the time. I felt her pain. I told her that she could make it on her own with support from other people who would help. She had to believe in herself that she could do this. She, with her two children, got an apartment. I went to see how she was doing. She said she was thinking of moving back with her husband again. "The kids are hungry. The welfare isn't enough to feed and buy clothes for them. He will kill me if he finds me." She was crying out of control.

"He'll kill you if you do go back. Give it some more time. It will get easier," I told her. I think she may have gone back. I never heard from her again.

I called my brother David in Maine to tell him where I was. I had stayed in contact with him since I moved back to New Hampshire. I had gone down on a weekend twice to visit. He was upset but I told him not to worry. I didn't want to involve the family. I was afraid Eric might do something to my family if I went to stay there.

I rented a car in order to look for another car to buy. I found what seemed like a good deal on a car. I went to the credit union and they approved the loan that day. One of the men who worked at the car dealer agreed to bring the car to me the next day if I would drive him back. We met at the car rental where I returned the car.

After a couple of weeks of staying at the shelter I was settled down. I decided that I needed to go back to work again. Mary met me at a restaurant in a nearby town. I had found a cheap place to rent. It didn't sound like much but was worth checking out. We found the apartment building and went inside to talk to the person in charge of renting the rooms.

"Yes, I do have one room available. It has a hot plate, a small refrigerator, and a table with a chair. If you need another chair I could probably find one. The bathroom is just down the hall from your room."

I took the room. It was cheap but I didn't like the idea of having to share a bathroom with other people. I didn't plan to stay there a long time anyway, so I could live with that.

Mary helped me move in the few things I needed. She left afterward and I was there by myself. It wasn't so bad. I went to the store and got a few groceries and a bottle of wine. From a phone booth I called one of my co-workers and asked if I could ride to work with her and her husband the following morning. I didn't want to take any chances of Eric seeing me. He wouldn't be looking for me in their car.

"No problem. We'll be there in the morning," she said.

When I returned back to the apartment house, there was a man sitting out front on the steps.

"Hello," he said and nodded. "You must be the new girl who moved in upstairs."

"Yes I am," I said in reply.

"I live downstairs in the big apartment. Come on down after you get settled and I'll give you the lowdown on the people who live here."

I went up to my room and made a sandwich. I was just getting ready to go outside when someone was knocking on the door. I was scared to answer it, afraid Eric may have already found me.

"It's me, Carl. Was wondering if you want to come down for a beer? I'll show you another way to get up to your room."

"Okay."

I opened the door and followed Carl down the hall. "There's the bathroom and there is a lock on the inside. Make sure you lock it when you go in."

"Thanks. I'll do that."

We went outside through a back door and then from the outside into his apartment. His apartment was an average size. It was a one bedroom with private bath, living room, and full kitchen. He went to the refrigerator and got out two beers. "Hope you like Bud. That's what we all drink here."

"Yeah, that's fine."

"I've been living here for ten years. I was one of the first ones to move in here. I have seen a lot of people come and go. Most of the guys here stay for a short time. Most are divorced or have DUI's. There have been a few women move in, but they never stay long. Are you planning to stay very long?" Carl was staring at me and waiting for my answer.

I was glad that it was a weekly rental and small deposit. I only had to give a week's notice if I decided to move out.

"I'm really not sure. It depends on how things go," I told him.

"You work?"

"Yeah." I didn't want to reveal all the details to him about why I was there and where I worked.

"Been here long or you just move here?"

"About a year. I thought you were going to show me another way to get to my room." I changed the subject.

"Come on, I'll show you." He got up and went over by the bathroom. There was a door there and steps going upstairs. "At the top of the stairs is a door that goes into your room."

I wasn't sure I liked that. I would check to make sure there was a lock on the door from inside my room and that it was locked.

"You can come down to visit me from your room and no one would know," Carl told me.

"Great." I didn't plan to come down to visit. He seemed okay but I didn't know him.

I had the beer and told Carl that I was going back to my room. "I have to work tomorrow and need to get in bed. I will be leaving my car here in the parking lot. I am riding to work with a friend. No one will bother it, will they?"

"No, but I'll watch it for you," he was quick to say.

"Thanks for the beer." I went outside to the front door and up to my room.

The alarm system on the building evidently didn't work. One of the reasons why I wanted to rent a room here was for the security system. I would have to tell the landlady about it.

Mindy and her husband arrived in the morning to pick me up. I ducked down in the seat when we got closer to the place where we all worked. I didn't want to take any chances that Eric might see me.

It was Thursday and so far no signs of Eric.

Carl would see me come home in the evening and stop me to talk for a minute. He kept inviting me down for a beer but I kept putting him off. I would tell him that I had something to do. I had gone to the grocery store and on my return Carl stopped me as I was going in the front door.

"Come on down for a beer when you put your groceries up."

"Alright, give me a couple of minutes." It wouldn't hurt. I wanted some company anyhow, someone to talk to. It was lonesome sitting in the room with nothing but four walls to look at. I had no TV or radio, just four walls.

131

I went down to Carl's apartment through the secret door. He got us a beer. "What's that on the ceiling?" There were dark things all over the ceiling.

"I have allergies that I have to take medication for. That is why I don't work. I am on disability because of the extreme allergies. Those are boogers that I sling up there when the allergies are so bad," Carl told me.

I just laughed knowing he must be pulling my leg. I know he couldn't be telling me the truth. I kept looking up at the ceiling and thinking of what he said. I felt a little sick. I drank down the beer faster than planned so I could leave. I felt uneasy now and thoughts going through my head. Maybe Carl was a weirdo or something.

Carl came over and sat next to me on the couch. He tried to put his hand on my breast.

"Don't do that!" I yelled at him.

"I just want you to trust me. I'm not going to do anything. I want you to trust me, okay?"

"No!" I yelled at him again and got up. "I'm going to my room."

"Okay. I didn't mean to scare you. I wouldn't hurt you. I'll see you tomorrow. Just trust me," he said.

The next evening was Friday and I didn't have to work on Saturday, so I decided to take a chance and go out for a drink. I had seen a local bar not far away. I cleaned the bathroom before taking a shower. I made sure the door was locked and undressed. My shower was quick. I didn't want to be undressed long. I envisioned one of the men trying to break in and it made me nervous. I dressed quickly, grabbed my things, and went to my room. I had a mirror over the sink in my room so I could use that to put on make-up and use the sink to brush my teeth.

I had some cute outfits that I really liked to wear. I chose the one with the lavender slacks and matching knitted vest. A silk long-sleeved white blouse would look nice with the slacks and vest. I was ready to go. I got my purse and car keys and went outside. Several of the guys who lived there were sitting outside in chairs drinking beer. Carl was also outside but he wasn't sitting with the guys. He was sitting in front of his apartment in a chair by himself.

"Hi, how ya doing?" one of the guys asked.

"Good, how about yourself?" I answered as I walked by.

"Good. Good," the guy said.

Carl was watching me as I came in his direction. "Going out on the town? You dress preppy. You sure you want to go out? You might get in trouble."

"I'm just going out for a drink to get out for a while." I didn't feel like I should have to answer to him but said it to pacify him.

I had one drink at the bar and left. I wasn't comfortable there. There was no place else to go so I went back toward the house. When I pulled in the driveway, I saw that Carl was still sitting outside. The other guys were no longer outside. I really wanted to avoid him so I thought I would go in the back way. He saw me though.

"Trying to avoid me?" I heard Carl say.

"No, just going up to my room."

"Come sit with me for a minute and have a beer."

I guessed it wouldn't hurt. I went over to where he was now standing.

"Come on in and I'll get you a beer," he said.

I followed him inside but realized that I only had one cigarette. "I'll be back in a minute. I'm out of cigarettes. Let me go get a pack and I'll be right back." I also wanted to unlock the door in my room that led up from Carl's apartment. I wouldn't have to walk back around the house to get to my room. I went back down the stairs to Carl's. Carl let me in and handed me a beer.

"Well, did you have a good time out?" Carl wanted to know.

"It was boring," I told him.

Carl sat beside me on the couch. It made me nervous. I wondered if he would try to touch my breast again. He told me that I didn't want to get involved with any of the guys staying there, that they were losers. He said he could keep me safe if I just trusted him.

I didn't trust him and I felt very uncomfortable. I couldn't believe what Carl said next to me.

"If I make love to you, you had better not give me a disease."

"I think I need to leave." I got up and headed for the stairs but Carl stopped me.

"You don't trust me yet?" He had a grip on my arm and I couldn't get away.

"No, I don't trust you. Let go of me! I want to go to my room!" I pulled free of his grip and ran up the stairs with him behind me. I got inside and locked the door. My heart was beating so fast. I checked the other lock on the main door to make sure it was locked too.

Carl was at the stairs door. "Let me in, Diane, I won't hurt you. Come on. I didn't mean anything by what I said."

"Go away and leave me alone," I said to Carl. It got quiet. I had to go to the bathroom but was afraid to go outside the door. I could hold it for a while to make sure Carl didn't come back to my door. About ten minutes had passed and I knew I had to go to the bathroom. I was about to open the door when Carl was knocking at the front door of my room.

"Diane, just open the door and we will talk. I don't want you to think that I am a bad person."

"Just let it go for now. I'll talk to you tomorrow. It's just me. Not your fault." I thought if I could convince him that it wasn't him who had the problem he would leave.

"You're not lying, are you?" he asked.

"No, I'm not lying." I was still afraid to open the door and go to the bathroom so I used a plastic bowl that I had in my room instead. I wouldn't go out until the morning.

In the morning I got dressed and left to go to a phone booth to call Mary. "I have to get out of there. I am afraid to stay there any longer."

Mary said she would be there shortly. We talked to the landlady but told her the reason that I wanted to move was because I was afraid to stay there with no security system. I thought since Carl had lived there so long, she may not believe me. The landlady gave me back my deposit and Mary and I packed up my things.

Carl was watching us from outside his apartment. He asked, "Are you leaving?"

"Yes, I am," I replied.

I moved back in with Mary. With having a different car, Eric didn't find me for a while. Once he knew I was back staying at Mary's, he sent flowers and said he loved me on the note. He called her house

asking for me but I refused to talk to him. Mary and I both started
receiving flowers from him. He was trying to get to me through her.
Mary almost begged me, "Why don't you just talk to him? Maybe then
he won't call all the time."

"You don't know him the way I do. I don't ever want to talk to him
again," I replied.

"He sends you flowers all the time and he probably does love you.
Maybe this time would be better." Mary kept trying to get me to give
in.

I realized that he was getting to her and she was getting tired of the
phone ringing all the time.

The phone rang. I only answered the phone when no one else was
there to answer it. I knew it was probably Eric. "Hello," I said.

"Honey, baby. God, I've missed you. I want to see you. Will you
see me?" He was crying so hard I could hardly understand a word he
was saying.

"Why don't you stop calling here all the time? I would have talked
to you already if I had wanted to."

"I know you got another car. I saw you the other day." Now he
sounded like the asshole he was.

"So what?" I said. "I don't care that you know I got another car. I
wasn't trying to hide it."

His voice was quiet now. "Just see me. Come to my place. You
didn't think I could get my own place, did you? I want you to see it.
It is nice."

My mind was in motion for a minute before I could answer him.
"That's great. How long you been there?"

"Three weeks. Come see it. I promise we will talk and if you want
I will go get some wine for you. I know what kind you like. I'm not
drinking anymore. I quit! Will you come? I'll give you directions."

Maybe if I did go, he would be proud enough of himself to stay
there, if I said it was nice. "Okay. I'll come."

It was a motel room with a kitchenette. It had been turned into a
weekly rental place. "This is nice, Eric. This is all you need living by
yourself."

"You could stay here with me, you know."

135

I wondered how long before he would ask that. It turned out all right. We talked like we hadn't seen each other for ages. Eric was trying not to say the wrong thing to scare me off. He wanted to have sex but I refused and started to leave.

"Stay longer. We don't have to make love. I've missed you so much and just wanted you."

I ignored him, trying to change the subject. "I'm proud of you. You could get some nice curtains put up with a matching color spread for the bed. I could make you some things to put on the walls." I hoped that would encourage him to want to stay there alone.

I had to find a place to live too. I knew of a mobile home that would be for rent in September, though I didn't want to wait until then to move out of Mary's. I knew of a campground nearby and thought if I could get a tent and an air mattress, I could stay there for the summer. I got everything set up at the campground and checked on the mobile home to make sure that I could rent it.

Eric wanted to stay at the campground with me. He insisted it wasn't safe for a woman to stay there alone. He said if he stayed there he could save enough money to pay the rent and deposit on the mobile home that he hoped we could rent together. "Let me pay for it," he said.

With him not drinking maybe he would be better, and I was afraid to stay at the campground by myself. I let Eric stay with me there. Everything went good for most of the summer, but then the arguing started again.

"If you would marry me like you said, I wouldn't be so upset. All I want is you to be my wife again. I haven't been drinking and I will never hit you again, I promise."

How many times had I heard that story before? If I did marry him again, it would buy me more time. I could play the game longer if I had to.

We got married by a justice of the peace in Seabrook, New Hampshire. We moved into the mobile home in the fall, like we planned. Eric was getting out of control and I knew he was drinking again. I suggested that he go to Alcoholics Anonymous to get help. He got very defensive and started beating on me, claiming that it was all my fault. I went along and agreed with him.

136

"Yes, I guess you're probably right. It's all my fault. I have put you through so much. I will try harder to be a better wife to you."

Eric looked surprised and said, "Good, I'm glad you finally realized that."

Eric was now driving a fuel truck for a company across the border in Maine. A co-worker of mine had told me that the company was looking for a driver. Her husband's parents owned the company. I kept praying he would have an accident and he would get burned up if the fuel exploded. When I would hear on the news of such an accident, I would stop what I was doing to listen, in hopes that I would get lucky.

Eric came to where I worked one day looking for me, but I had already left. I had to leave early to get to the bank to put money in my safe deposit box. He had a gun and demanded to see me. He didn't believe them when they told him at the plant that I had already left. The plant manager called the police. I was not aware of what had happened until the next day. Eric didn't say a word to me that evening. He didn't even seem upset.

The next morning when I walked into the plant, took off my jacket and started to work, I felt eyes looking at me. Mary came to me and said, "Let's go to the break room and talk." I thought I had done something wrong.

Mary got us a cup of coffee and we sat at one of the tables. She began, "Joyce feels that you need to find another job. After yesterday, the company feels someone could get hurt or killed. They can't have this going on at the company. She said you can just quit and if you can't find a job right away, you can collect unemployment for a few weeks."

I had no idea what she was talking about. "What happened yesterday? No one said anything to me. What's going on?"

She looked shocked. "You mean Eric didn't tell you?"

"Tell me what?" Mary told me what had happened. I was beyond angry, I was irate.

I said good-bye to all my friends at the plant. Some of us cried together. Joyce and the plant manager came in to our department and wished me luck. They told me how sorry they were that I had to leave.

I left there and bought a newspaper. I saw several places where they were hiring. I filled out applications for the better part of the day. I told Eric that I had left my job because they were getting slow and was afraid of a lay-off. He really thought he was getting something over on me. I got a call two days later to start work at a place where they made glue guns. The pay wasn't very good but it was steady.

I worked with a woman at my new job whose husband was an alcoholic. He beat her and was mean to the kids. She was scared to leave him but she knew she would have to do something soon. We talked about our husbands all the time, during breaks.

I went to the grocery store after work my first day at my new job to get something to make for supper. I ran into the manager of the apartment building where I had lived before. She asked, "How you doing? You aren't still involved with that man, are you?"

I briefly explained what had been going on. I told her that I didn't know where to go to get away from him so he couldn't find me.

"Disappear!" she said out of the blue. "Just disappear. Take only what you need and leave the rest. Don't be in touch with any, I mean any, friends or family for about a year. I know that sounds hard and scary but I had to do it. I went through the same thing you are. It worked. He gave up looking after a while."

"Where would I go?" I asked.

"They have shelters for battered women all over the country. You could call one locally. They will give you the names and numbers of shelters, and directions. It's frightening to be out there all alone but it's the only way."

I thanked her for giving me that advice and information. She wished me luck.

I told my friend at work, Beth, what the woman had told me. Beth said that she would make some calls to find locations and directions. She said she had some maps at home that she would give me if I wanted. Beth had gotten some information for me so I started making some plans. Beth kept the maps and information for me. She said when I was ready to leave, call her and she would meet me somewhere and give me the papers and maps.

I told my supervisor what was going on. He said he understood why I felt I had to do this, especially since Eric had come there to work several times to get money from me. He thought Eric was rude and disgusting, the way he talked to me.

Eric started going up to the dog track betting on dogs. The track was a half-mile from the house. I knew he was losing money there. He came home one afternoon with a fat lip and dents in the truck that he had bought recently. I asked him, "What happened, Eric?"

"Some guy tried to run me off the road as I was coming out of the dog track so I got him to stop and busted him in the mouth. No, I didn't lose any money. I know that's what you're thinking."

I could see the evil in his eyes. "Looks like he got one in too." I almost laughed but knew that would just provoke him.

"Yeah, but you should have seen him."

In the morning before I left for work, Eric asked me if I had any money. He said he didn't get his regular fuel check yet that week and needed money for fuel. "I'll get it today," he stated.

I gave him twenty dollars. "That's all I've got but need it back. That was money I was going to buy some stuff with at the store. If I don't get it back, we won't eat tonight." I had more money but I wanted to make him think that was all I had. He would get something to eat before he came home so he wasn't worried about eating if he didn't pay me back. He wouldn't worry if I ate or not.

That evening after work, I stopped by the store and got some bread for a sandwich. I figured if he didn't pay back the money, I would say that I just had enough for loaf of bread. I knew I would have something to eat. I waited and waited but no Eric. What was holding him up? I didn't really care if he came home or not, but hoped for the worst for him and the best for me. Maybe he went to the track again or stopped off for a beer. It was hard to say with him. I just hoped he didn't come home in a pissy mood if his day didn't go just right.

Seven o'clock the phone rang. It was Eric. He had been arrested for driving under the influence. "Come and bail me out of this hellhole. I will sue these bastards. They said I had been drinking but I hadn't been. They can't get away with this. Call my boss and tell them that I got held up and then come bail me out."

He was desperate. Someone was actually keeping him in jail. I took the phone away from my mouth, fearing that he may hear me laughing. I was so amused. I had to straighten out so I could continue to talk to him. I said, "Eric, you know I don't have the money to get you out. Even if I did, I can't use it for that. Got bills to pay."

"You better get here and bail me out. You can get the money somehow. If you don't, you'll be one sorry bitch when I get my hands on you." Eric sounded like he could have killed me right over the phone.

"I'll be there as soon as I can get the money," I lied.

I called his boss and told them where he was and what had happened. "We'll bail him out and get our truck. He no longer has a job. We'll get our money back from what we owe him. Shouldn't do it but want him away from us and the company before something else more serious happens."

I begged her, "Please wait until I can pack some things real quick and get out of here." She agreed. I tried to call Beth but got no answer. I wasn't sure where to go and really needed the papers and maps she had. I didn't want to stay in the area that night. I wanted to get away.

It was snowing. There was already about an inch of accumulation. I headed for Maine. I drove out in the country hoping to find a motel that had a vacancy. Four hours later, I found one. It was nice to get in a hot shower and relax. I called Beth and asked if we could meet the next day.

She said, "Sure thing."

It had been snowing all night. The roads were covered in snow. It was early but I had to get going. I met with Beth and got the information I needed. She gave me the phone number of Jim, the supervisor where I had been working. She said he wanted me to call after I was safe so he would know that I was all right. Although I was afraid Eric would see me, I had to get to the bank. I had to get all my money and the other valuables that I had put in the safety deposit box. I also had to close out my checking account. After leaving the bank I went to the police station and told them what I had planned to do. I asked them to help me. One of the officers escorted me back to the mobile home.

Eric's truck was gone so I knew he must have gotten out of jail. I was afraid he would come back so the officer told me he would wait until I got all that I wanted from the home. Eric came down the road in his truck while I was there. He must have seen the officer's vehicle sitting there and it discouraged him from stopping. As I was loading things in my car, the officer asked me if Eric had any outstanding warrants that I knew of. I told him that I thought he had one in Maryland for stealing tires. He made some phone calls to the station but came up empty. He was trying to find a reason to detain him, to keep him from following me when I left.

I got the car packed up with clothes, personal papers, and anything I thought I would need to get by with. I hated to leave my furniture, TV, stereo, and everything else that belonged to me. "It all can be replaced," someone had told me. "Your safety is more important."

"Where you headed? This blizzard is going to be bad to drive in. You be real careful and if it gets too bad, stop someplace," the officer said to me. He was really a nice person.

"I'm headed for Florida," I told him.

"I can follow you to the state line, but then I am out of my jurisdiction. I'll call in to the Massachusetts police and tell them what's going on. It will be up to them whether they want to ride behind you for a few miles, to make sure he's not following you."

I felt better already. Eric passed us the road headed toward the house. I watched to see if he turned around or not. He didn't. I had taken some dish towels and coffee mugs that were still wrapped in Christmas paper with me. They were for some friends who lived in Maine. It was the 28th of December and I had hoped to go to Maine to see family and friends before Christmas, but I didn't get there. By taking the gifts, I hoped that Eric would think that was where I was going. If he did then he wouldn't follow me. He would wait to see if I returned in a few days, and if not, he would drive to Maine to find me.

I had a Massachusetts police officer behind me for a long time. He stayed some distance back and in the blizzard I couldn't see him all the time. I couldn't drive very fast. I was blinded by the snow blowing, and the snow was mounting quickly. My nerves were on edge. I wanted to stop but I kept going. I felt the farther away I was, the better I would feel. It was getting dark. I started looking for a place to stop for the night.

I could barely drive in the parking lot of the motel with all the snow. I checked in and asked the front desk person where the closest grocery store was. I had to get something to eat and drink. I hadn't had anything all day.

I found the grocery store even in all the snow. A young man working in the store asked me what in the world I was doing out in the blizzard. "I'm on my way to Florida but got held up here because of the snow. Had to get something to eat." He suggested one of their burgers. They had a microwave there in the store to heat it. I got the burger, some chips and a Coke.

Back at the room, I ate, made plans for traveling the next day and made a phone call. Kimberly, Eric's sister-in-law, and I had talked after we had stayed there those few days. She had told me that Eric had tried to force her to have sex with him when her husband wasn't home. Eric had stayed with them for a short time years ago when Kimberly and Josh were first married. "I hate him. I don't trust him at all. He even tried to make problems with Josh and me. How can you stand to be with such a liar?" Kimberly and Josh said if I ever needed a place to stay, I was welcome to come there. When I called them that night, Kimberly answered the phone.

"Hello?"

"Kimberly, hi, it's Diane. How you doing?"

"Good, good." I knew I could trust them but was still skeptical of giving out to much information.

"I'm close to your house but wanted to call you before I came."

"Are you alone?"

"Yeah, I left Eric." I waited for a positive response.

"I'm glad you did. You can stay here. I'll give you directions. When are you coming?"

"Have you heard from Eric?" I was curious to see if he was calling around to see if anyone had heard from me or not. I thought if he had been worried that I wasn't coming back, he would have been on the phone, crying to everyone that I left him.

"Nope, haven't heard a thing. I don't think he'd think you would come here, do you?"

"No, I don't think so. He doesn't know that you and I talked. He probably thinks I went to Maine, so he won't be in too big of a hurry to find me. He will party, eat all the food in the house and then look to see what I took. He thinks since I left all the furniture, TV and stereo that I will be back. He will have a rude awakening when he figures it out," I told Kimberly.

"I'd like to see his face when he tries to find you and realizes he can't. He will be in shock. What will he do without you to hold his hand? You have put up with more than I could have with him. I'd have killed him." She was angry.

"Believe me, that thought crossed my mind many times. He wasn't worth going to jail for." I was feeling good about doing what I was. She gave me directions to her house and promised that if Eric should call, they would tell him they hadn't heard from me.

I stayed at their house until January first. I was starting a new year. I planned to make it a good one. I decided to go to Florida by way of Ohio. I stopped to see Ester. She said she knew of someone who had an apartment where I could stay until I was ready to leave. I figured I could get a job, make more money and then leave. I worked for three weeks and saved all my money. I stayed well hidden all the time.

Dan's niece lived in Florida. She said I could stay with her if I came down. We had plans to split the rent if I stayed and got a job.

Debbie, the manager of the apartment building where I stayed, was really nice to me. She offered to do my laundry while I was at work. She said I needed a massage and said she would give me one. "No thanks. I'd rather a man had his hands on me if you don't mind," I said. She was annoyed. Maybe I hurt her feelings. She was just being nice, I guess. We spent almost every evening together talking. There was something about her that I was a little uncomfortable with but couldn't put my finger on. I told Ester that I was a little uneasy with Debbie but it was probably because I never really had any real girlfriends.

Neither one of us had ever been to Florida. We wanted to go to Disney World and Debbie had never seen the ocean. Her mom paid for her plane fare to fly back home.

143

Reservations were made in Statesville, North Carolina, for our first night. We had planned to drive seven or eight hours each day. It was ten o'clock when we got into Statesville. After checking in at the motel, we went to find a place to eat. Nothing was open. I asked at a convenience store where we could find a place to eat. "The Holiday Inn serves food in the bar. They are open. The Waffle House is open too." I thanked the woman for the information. We decided on the Holiday Inn. We were both ready for a drink along with something to eat.

The place was pretty full. There were a couple of guys in there being loud and having a good time. I asked the bartender about ordering food. She gave us a menu and then took our order. I ordered a cheeseburger and fries and Debbie got a club. While waiting for our food, we ordered a drink. I got a whiskey sour. It tasted good after the long drive.

I noticed that the guys that were being so loud were looking at us. An older gentleman, real tall and thin, came over to our table. "Can I buy you girls a drink?" Before we could reply, he asked, "Y'all from around here?" Wow! We were really in the South. I had never heard a southern accent before in person, just on TV.

"Well, no. I'm from Maine and she's from Ohio," I answered. I hoped he hadn't forgotten the drinks. He went over to the bar and ordered drinks. The bartender brought them to our table. The other guy who he had been cutting up with came over to our table as well.

"Just come in tonight? Where you headed? My name is Henry and this is Bill. He lives in Alabama. He's up here on business." I thought, *This man is a talker*. He seemed nice. "Mind if we sit down?" I looked at Debbie. She didn't act as though she really wanted them to but she said nothing.

"Go ahead, have a seat." I liked listening to them talk. Our food was brought to us.

"What're your names?" Bill asked. "We told you ours."

"I'm Diane and this is Debbie," I said.

Henry then spoke up, "Buy you a drink if you can guess how old I am." He was looking at me.

"Forty-two," I guessed, but really thought he was older.

"You owe me a drink, I'm forty-nine."

"Are you really? You don't look that old," I lied to him. We ate our food while talking to the two men. I liked Henry. He was fun. It was nice to laugh again.

We danced with the music from the jukebox. I really didn't know how to dance. I had just learned the disco with Darren. This was what they called beach music. Country music was also playing. I liked country music but didn't know how to dance to it.

Later that evening, Henry and Bill wanted us to go to the Waffle House with them. I wasn't hungry but wanted to try some grits.

Henry asked if we wanted to stay one more day. He said he would take us shopping and out to see the town. I was in no big hurry to get to Florida, I was enjoying myself here. Debbie didn't want to stay. I tried to talk her into it but she still wanted to leave. Henry called at eight in the morning to see if we were still staying. I told him we were, thinking I could still convince Debbie to stay. She wanted to leave. We packed up the car and got on Interstate 40, headed for Florida.

I stopped at a rest area to call Henry. He had given me his phone number. I felt bad that we had left without letting him know. I didn't have the courage to call so we went on.

We checked into the motel where we had reservations. We were both excited to go see the sights. I called Dan's niece to let her know we were there. I told her that we were going to Disney World the next day, but the day after we would come to her apartment.

Debbie and I were arguing like we were married to each other or something. I thought she acted more like a boyfriend than a girlfriend. She always wanted to touch me or rub my back.

We went to Disney World. I really enjoyed it. Debbie complained that her leg was hurting her so we went back to the room. I wondered why she acted the way she did. "Debbie, are you gay?" I had to find out because it bothered me.

"I'm bi-sexual," she said.

"Why didn't you tell me this before? Don't think you're touching me." I felt betrayed. I wished that she had told me before we came down here together. I had never met anyone who was bi. I was so uncomfortable around her from then on.

145

We went to Dan's niece's apartment the next day. The following day, I took Debbie to the airport to fly back to Ohio. I was looking for a job in the newspaper. I had no idea of the location of these jobs. I had hoped that Dan's niece would be helpful to me but she wasn't.

Chapter 10

Living in the South

I called Henry from Florida. I told him that I would be coming through North Carolina again on my way back to Ohio. I apologized for leaving like we had, and said that I had really wanted to stay there that extra day.

It was hot in Florida. I was used to the cold so this was wonderful weather. I only had to wear a t-shirt instead of the usual sweatshirt for a change. I already loved the South. I wanted to get started on my trip back. I left Dan's niece a note and told her that I was going back to Ohio. It was too aggravating looking for a job with no one to help you find your way around the area. I had made some long distance calls and left her some money. I said if that didn't cover the bill to let me know through Dan and I would make it good.

I really wanted to get back to North Carolina but I had been driving for several hours and I was tired. In Georgia, I stopped at a motel and got a room for the night. I could have driven the rest of the way that night but wanted to see Henry when I was refreshed and not so tired. I called Henry from the room and we made plans to meet at the Waffle House the next morning. I didn't sleep very well that night; I was anxious to get to North Carolina again.

I had no problem finding the exit that Henry had told me to take. The Waffle House wasn't far from the exit. I felt somewhat uneasy walking into the restaurant alone, only just seeing Henry the one time before. Henry was sitting with a friend drinking coffee, but when he saw me, he looked up, got up and came over to me. Henry steered me to the booth where he had been sitting.

"Want some coffee or something to eat?" Henry asked me.

"Maybe coffee," I answered him.

"How was your trip here? Didn't get lost, did you?"

"No," I answered quickly.

Henry's friend, Joe, got up from the booth. "Well, I got to go. Some people have to work for a living. Nice meeting you," Joe said as he departed.

Henry began telling me of different motels around the area. He said when we finished coffee he would have me follow him to a motel where I could stay for however many days I would choose to stay. It was a chain motel that I was familiar with it. I checked into the room and Henry followed me in, carrying my bags.

"I have some work to do for a couple of hours, but I'll be back around five and we can go out to eat," Henry was saying as he walked to the door. "Oh, I'll have my boys with me, if that's okay?"

"All right. See ya later." Although I was nervous about meeting his boys, I wanted to see Henry.

Henry was back before five to pick me up. Rick was nine and John was eleven. They were showing off and checking me out for approval. We ate at a fish place. They called it a fish camp, but I didn't understand why. The food was good and there was plenty of it. After dinner Henry took me back to the motel and said he would call me in the morning.

The next morning he called early. "Want to come over to the house today? Maybe we can do something this evening. The boys will be going back to their mom's house this evening."

"Yeah, sure. What time will you be here?" I thought I might find a store or go looking around the area if he wasn't coming to pick me up until later.

"As soon as you are ready. I want to see you." His voice sounded anxious.

"Give me an hour to get ready then." I wanted to see him too.

Henry had a nice home that he rented. It had a spiral staircase down into the basement. He used to own a log house but sold it after he and his wife separated. We hung around the house and talked for a while, first about him and then about me. He told me of his new separation and soon divorce from his wife. He said he had visitation with the boys. I told him of my bad experience with Eric and that I wasn't looking to get back in a serious relationship with anyone for now.

We decided to go out to eat later and go by the Holiday Inn to have a couple of drinks afterward. I asked Henry to take me back to the room so I could shower and change before we went out. I wanted to look good for him.

Henry returned in about an hour in a suit. He looked sharp. I felt like I wasn't dressed as well as he was, with just dress slacks, a blouse and a vest. He said I looked fine. We ate at a Japanese steakhouse. We then went to the Holiday Inn and talked over a couple of drinks.

"I'm going to have to head for Ohio tomorrow early. I saw on the weather there is a big storm coming in. I don't want to run into bad weather on my way there," I told Henry.

"I was hoping you could stay a couple more days," he said.

"I need to get back and see if I can find a job. Money is running low and I have bills to pay," I said.

"You can ride a lawnmower, can't you? I'll give you a job working with me. You could stay at my house." I knew he didn't want me to leave but I knew I had to.

I didn't answer him on that one. Besides, it was February. How much grass could you cut in February? I had never ridden a riding mower, and furthermore, I didn't want to move in with someone I barely knew. What conditions would there be and how much control would he have over me? I felt like I should just go back to Ohio and we could keep in contact, maybe see each other from time to time.

The phone rang in my room first thing in the morning. Henry wanted me to meet him for breakfast before I left. We met again at the Waffle House.

"You sure you don't want to stay? Call me as soon as you get back to Ohio so I'll know you made it there all right, okay? You got my phone number, right?"

"Yes, I got your number. I'll call you as soon as I get there," I said as I was getting in my car.

While driving back to Ohio the fear was creeping back in me. What if Eric had gone to Ohio and was looking for me there? Where would I stay when I got there? All these negative thoughts were running through my head. As I got closer to the town in Ohio I got really nervous. The storm was now here and the snow was falling heavily. I checked in a motel room for the night. I immediately called Henry to let him know that I arrived here safely.

"How's the weather? You get there before the storm did?" Henry wanted to know.

"I ran into the storm about 30 miles before I got here but it wasn't bad until I got here. I got a room for the night. I'm going to make some phone calls after I talk to you and see if I can stay with a friend here while looking for a job. I have the local paper with me. I'll look at it tonight."

"Still think you should come back here and work for me," he said. "What if you can't find a job there? How long are you going to stay if you can't find a job?" Henry was putting the questions to me.

"I really don't know. I have to find something soon. I'll just have to see how it goes this next week. Let me get off the phone so I can make some calls." I needed to know if I had someplace to stay the next night or not.

"Can I call you later? Are you going to be there? What time would be good to call?" More questions from Henry.

"Call me about nine if that's not too late. I should know something by then." I gave him the number there in the room and got off the phone. I called a friend that I had met prior to leaving for Florida. His name was Denny and he lived with his mom. He was a few years younger than I was.

"Hi, Denny. How you doing? This is Diane. I didn't stay in Florida and now I'm back in town. I'm looking for a job again and need a place to stay until I find something and a place to rent. Any chance your mom would let me stay there for a few days or maybe a week?" I held my breath while he went to ask her.

"She said if you were willing to pay twenty dollars a week you could stay," Denny said.

"Yeah, sure. I didn't want to stay for nothing. Great! I'll be there sometime tomorrow. Thanks, Denny." I felt better already. Now I just had to find a job.

Henry called me at nine that evening. I told him I had a place to stay while looking for a job. He wanted to know if I was staying with another man. I explained to him that it was his mom's house and I would be sleeping in my own room and not with Denny. He sounded disappointed that I had a place to stay. I gave him the number at Denny's so he could call me if he wanted to.

Several feet of snow had fallen during the night, so it took me a while to dig the car out so I could go get something to eat and go to Denny's. Henry had already called there for me so I asked if I could call him back. Denny's mom said it was okay.

"Hi, Henry. You called here for me?"

"Didn't know how soon before you would be there. Any luck with jobs yet?" he wanted to know.

"Haven't had the time to call anywhere yet. I'm getting ready to now. Call me later this evening if you want. I should have some idea of what is available for jobs. Talk to you later." I knew he hoped that I wouldn't find anything so it would force me to go back there. It might come to that. I might have to go back there.

I looked in the paper, made calls and asked people of any jobs they knew of. Henry continued to keep in contact and I continued to give him the news of no luck with a job. He finally said to me after a week, "Just come back. You can look for a job here and stay at the house. It won't cost you anything. I have two bedrooms. When the boys are here, they can sleep with me. How's that sound?"

"Let me think about it. If I haven't found anything by tomorrow, I'll call you and we can discuss it further." I wanted to go back but didn't know if that was the right thing to do. I would need my own space and I didn't want him telling me what to do. I was not sure I would be able to deal with the boys either. I could go back, and if it didn't work out I would get my own place.

The next day I called Henry and told him I was on my way back to North Carolina. I called him again when I was about an hour away from Statesville. "I'll be there in about an hour."

He gave me directions where to meet him so I wouldn't get lost, in a K-Mart parking lot. As soon as I pulled in the parking lot I saw his Bronco. Henry was standing outside leaning against his vehicle. He walked quickly to my car, leaned over and gave me a kiss. "Come on. Follow me," he said.

I started looking for a job the next day. It wasn't much, but I got a job at one of the local motels cleaning rooms. I worked there for a month, then I got another job at a motel cleaning the halls and lobby, and when I was lucky, I got to do some room service. The tips from doing room service were usually good. It was a nicer motel and the pay was better than the other motel.

In the evening I went outside Henry's house and sat on the steps. It was so nice to be able to go outside in early March. It was actually warm. I was afraid to sit out long, afraid Eric might find me if he rode by. The phone would ring late at night and wake everybody up. No one would be on the other end. I started to sleep in the living room in a chair, so I could quickly answer the phone before it woke the boys and Henry. I would pick it up and put it back down until it would stop. I would finally go to bed and sleep what little bit I could. I'd often be awakened by Henry during the night when I had nightmares. He would hear me crying or shouting, he'd say, in the night.

I had been reading the paper and looking through the help wanted ads, and I came across a job similar to the one that I had in New Hampshire. I called and went for an interview. I was hired immediately.

Things went well for a while until we had problems with Henry's wife. She found out that I was staying at his house. Henry started getting letters from her attorney threatening to take his visitation rights away from him. I started staying with Henry's mom on the weekends when the boys were to be with Henry. I was feeling like a criminal and that I had no choice where I stayed. The fight continued for a while, then calmed down when we found out that she, too, was seeing someone. It was not easy having the boys there when Henry had visitation. I wasn't sure this was something that I wanted to do. Henry said to me one day when I felt like I had just had enough of the boys, the wife and the whole situation, "If I were in your shoes I would be long gone. There is no way I would put up with what you have been putting up with. I don't want you to leave but I couldn't blame you if you did."

I felt sorry for him. The boys were so young and Henry was an older father; it was hard for him. He had been through so much with the marriage and had lost so much. He always did a lot of small things for the boys so they would want to be with him. He was afraid of them not wanting to see him, wanting to stay with their mom all the time. He was always trying to make me happy and keep the boys happy too.

Rick wanted a dog so Henry got him a puppy. It was a Pomeranian. His name was Freddie. He had a doghouse outside and stayed there most of the time, but got to come in the house sometimes. He was cute but no one paid that much attention to him.

I refused to go to his mother's on the weekends when the boys were there now. I felt that if I had to do this, then I would get my own place. We slept in separate rooms, though. One morning I was awakened by a yell from Henry. The boys were also awake. Henry was sleeping in the bunk bed with Rick and the bed was not long enough for him. Henry was six foot two. He went to get up and caught his toe in the railing at the bottom of the bed. He had broken his toe. He had decided to give me the room with the bigger bed because it had air conditioning. There was a window air conditioner in the living room which he kept on to help keep the other bedroom cooler. Sometimes he and the boys would pull the mattresses off the beds and put them on the floor in the living room to keep even cooler when it was really hot.

We decided to buy a house. Henry asked if I was willing to help make the payments. I agreed. We went looking at mobile homes and decided on one with three bedrooms. Both the boys would have their own rooms. I told Henry that if I was helping to buy this home, we would share the master bedroom. There would be no more sleeping in separate rooms when the boys were home. They would just have to get used to it. We had been together a year now.

One night, shortly after moving in to the house, Eric called. Henry answered the phone. He gave me the phone. "Someone wants to talk to you." Henry was all ears and the boys were listening too. Eric said he knew that we had moved and that he wanted to know if I had any income tax papers that belonged to him.

"I have nothing of yours! Don't call me anymore!" I screamed.

Eric continued to ramble on about something and I was about to hang up the phone when Henry asked if it was Eric. "Yes," I replied.

"Just lay the phone down. He'll get tired of talking after a while."

I laid the phone down on the floor and walked away. You could hear him yelling across the room.

"Hello. Hello. Is anybody there? There's nobody there," we heard Eric saying.

Henry ran over to the phone and picked it up. "Now let me tell you something, you baldheaded son-of-a-bitch. If you want to see Diane, I'll buy you a bus ticket here. I would love for you to come here. Come on! Come on down here."

The boys were in hysterics laughing. I actually started laughing, too. We didn't hear from Eric for a while. Our second divorce had already become final.

Henry asked me to marry him and I said yes. The date was set for February 14, 1989. We would go to South Carolina and get married at a wedding chapel in one of the small towns. A friend of ours had made the arrangements. We would go the night before the wedding and come back the day of the wedding. Rick wanted to go but we felt that we would have a problem with his now ex-wife letting him. John was upset that we were getting married and threatened not to come back home if we went ahead with our plans. Rick, on the other hand, was all for it. Rick was wild and hard to control, but I understood him better than I did John. Rick was so much like his dad, and built like him too. He was tall, skinny, and had long arms and legs. He was so awkward. After we got back from South Carolina, Henry was worried about John not coming home again. "Just leave him alone, he'll come around," I told him. John decided that it hadn't done any good to threaten, so he came back home on the next visitation day.

John decided that he wanted to come and live with us all the time. I thought there must be something wrong for the complete change in him. He had found out that his mom was seeing someone now. He was really upset. Henry wanted to go for joint custody of both the boys. I didn't think that was something I could handle. That caused complications for us. It wasn't easy to adjust to, but I did the best I could.

Eric called again one Saturday afternoon at the house. "Let me tell you something," I said, "I have made a lot of mistakes in my life but the biggest mistake that I ever made was the day I got involved with you. Don't ever call here again." I hung up the phone. I never gave him a chance to say anything. I was afraid he would call back again, but he didn't.

Henry made good money, and he liked to spend it too. I had a new car and he had a new truck. We had money to go on vacation with and to buy things we wanted. The boys knew that both parents made good money and they both took advantage, always wanting the most expensive things. I didn't think they always needed things but they got what they wanted most of the time.

Henry also had a cleaning service, so when he wasn't cutting grass or it was too cold to work outside he had the cleaning to help bring in the money. He had several places that he cleaned. All the places had to be cleaned at night once or twice a week or on Saturday if it was one of the churches. I helped him do some of the cleaning and also helped him cut grass after work.

My sister Angie called one night to tell me that Dad had a growth on his chest the size of half a grapefruit. She said he hadn't been to the doctor but she told him she was going to take him. After taking Dad and having a biopsy done, the doctors confirmed that it was cancer. He was scheduled to go in the hospital to have it surgically removed. Dad had to go on chemo and have some radiation treatments. He was sick most of the time while having the treatments. The doctors felt they had gotten all the cancer.

I wanted to go see Dad in Maine. It had been several years since I had been back home and I missed the family. It was November now and I knew it would be cold there that time of year, so I told Henry to pack warm clothes and I did the same.

Daddy looked good and he said he felt good now that the treatments were done. The families decided to all go out to eat with Dad. There weren't a lot of choices to eat out at this time of year. Restaurants closed up after the tourist left. We decided on Chinese food; that particular restaurant was open all year round. I asked Dad if he liked Chinese food and he replied by saying, "I've never had

Chinese food, but I can be a Chinaman for one day, I guess." He still had a sense of humor. He ate everything on his plate even though complaining that his stomach hurt before he had finished. "I don't want anything to go to waste," he said.

Next month was Christmas and I hadn't gotten Dad anything. I asked him if there was anything he wanted or needed while I was there. He said he would really like to have a fan to put in the window. Daddy said he didn't get much breeze coming in through the windows in the summer. Henry and I went to look for a fan. Fans are not very easy to find in the wintertime in Maine. We did find one at one of the more popular stores in Ellsworth. Dad was very pleased and appreciative of the gift.

Several months later Dad was not feeling well. My sister Shari took Dad back to the doctor. They found more tumors in him but felt that they could only offer more treatments. Dad moved in with Shari so she could care for him. Dad died the following year, June 1990.

Henry's helpers in the landscaping business quit on him, so he had no one to help him work at the busiest time of the year. He asked me to take a leave of absence from my job to help him get caught up and until he could find someone to help him. We weren't very busy at the plant where I worked so they let me have the time off.

Henry had a bit of a temper, so it didn't take much to set him off most of the time. We were starting to argue. One Friday night after working all day we decided to go out to eat. We were almost at the restaurant and I said something to him that made him mad. He swung his arm across my face. I thought he had broken my nose. We ate quietly at the restaurant except for him saying, "You shouldn't have said that." The next morning when I got up and looked in the mirror, both my eyes were black. At the restaurant that we went to each morning before work, the other guys asked me what happened. I replied by saying, "Henry hit me." They looked at me and then at Henry. One of the guys spoke up and said, "Henry, you shouldn't have done that."

"I guess she won't say anything to me again," Henry replied.

I told Henry after a month of working with him that I was going back to my regular job. He didn't like that idea at all. I went in to take a shower and just as I got out, Henry threw a glass of cold water on me and said, "I can't believe you are quitting on me too." He finally talked me into quitting my regular job and working with him after continuously nagging and making me feel guilty.

After two years working with him, I couldn't take it anymore. I went back to my old job. Our relationship had already been hurt from working together.

I didn't feel like the house that we bought together was really mine, but more Henry's and the boys. Nothing I ever said or suggested meant much. Any final decisions Henry would make, and sometimes without my knowledge. I felt like I had to compete with the boys for everything, including attention.

John wanted a dog, a beagle puppy. John named him Chester. We had a small dog lot down back in the shade so the dogs stayed there during the day and were let out some to run after we got home from work. The boys didn't take care of the dogs so most of the time Henry had to. I wanted to get a dog, a Lab, but couldn't with the other two dogs. The dogs started running loose most of the time and sometimes the beagle would be gone for days. It had been several days and no Chester. Freddie was under the house barking at something and would not stop. Henry looked under the house to see what it was. It was Chester. Someone had shot him and he was dead. We buried him in the woods behind the house.

We started going to West Virginia to the dog track about once a month. I enjoyed doing that. There was a small bar and restaurant in one of the nearby towns that we had heard about. It was called Oogie's. They had poker machines and other fun machines to play. We would sit in there for hours playing the machines and having a few drinks. I hated it that we always lost but I knew we could still pay bills. Henry always had money stashed away for a rainy day so I knew not to worry.

The trips to the dog track starting to become more frequent and more expensive. When Henry wanted to go, I would sometimes try to talk him into doing something else or going someplace else for the weekend. He would give me a hard time and say I never wanted to do anything that he wanted to anymore. The gambling was getting out of control. He now was playing the poker machines in the local convenience stores. I played with him sometimes but only to get along with him, and I enjoyed it when I knew it was extra money and not bill money. It wouldn't have been so bad if he would have set a limit and then called it quits. It was getting to the point where the bills weren't being paid or were late. I tried to talk to him but he didn't hear a word I said. I threatened to leave him but he said I would lose everything. He said I would never be able to afford to make the car payment and we would have to sell the house and land. I felt like he wanted to stay in debt so I would never leave him. I would try to diet to get in better shape and he would say to me, "Trying to look good for your next boyfriend?" I knew that Henry was insecure and afraid of losing me and his boys.

We went out dancing often on Friday or Saturday night. One night when we returned back home late we got into an argument over something stupid. I told him that I felt I needed to leave. He was getting out of control. Henry hit me so hard that I fell, hitting the side of my head on the coffee table in the living room. I was knocked out. When I opened my eyes I was looking at the ceiling. I lay still for a few minutes, then started to get up, wondering where Henry was. He was asleep sitting up on the couch. In his hand he had my car keys. His own keys were in his pocket. I didn't dare try to get them, afraid that he would awake. I got my purse and quietly went to the door. I had no idea where I was going but I just started walking. I knew that I didn't want to be abused anymore. The old fears were back in my soul and my heart was racing. What if he woke and I was gone? Would he come looking for me?

I walked a mile or so with only oncoming traffic. I heard a car coming from behind so I hid in the trees on the side of the road. It was Henry. As soon as the car was out of sight I got back on the road. I ran as long as I could before I seen a car coming toward me. I literally jumped into the bushes to hide. It was our car. This continued for some time until I got to a place where there were no trees or bushes in which to hide. I hurried to get past that area but wasn't quick enough. Henry pulled up beside of me. My heart was in my throat. I opened the car door. He passed me a cup of coffee. "Here. This will warm you up. I am so sorry. I will never hurt you again. I have been looking for you for an hour. Come back home, please. I love you."

I was tired and didn't know what else to do at that point. I had heard that "I'll never hurt you again" so many times that it didn't mean a thing to me. I knew that it probably would never stop. I would have to do something, make some plans to get out of the situation.

I told Henry that I was going to get a Lab pup. "I really want a dog. We only have Freddie now. I will take care of it and train it." I looked in the paper for some Lab pups. Everyone I called had no more puppies left. I had seen an ad for Lab-mix puppies but didn't think I would be happy with a mix. "I want a purebred," I told Henry. He talked me into going to look at the puppies.

We found the house that had the puppies. The mother, a beautiful golden retriever, was outside when we arrived. The father was a black Lab that lived down the road. I still was not really enthusiastic about looking at the pups. As we got out of the car a woman approached us. "Hi," she said, "got some good-looking babies in here." We walked in the garage where the pups were.

"I really wanted a pedigreed black Lab. Which ones are female? I want one that is mostly black," I told the woman. As I was talking to her one of the pups kept crawling up on my feet. I would move just enough so the pup was no longer on my shoe but she would come right back again. I finally picked her up. "Is this a male or female?" I asked. A young boy had come out from the house into the garage by then.

"It's a female," the boy told me.

"She's mostly black, too," I said, getting more excited with the puppy. I felt that she picked me out to take her home. "I'll take her."

I had a box in the car to put her in for the ride home. She cried so I decided to hold her. She was only six weeks old. I named her Candy. She was so sweet. I already loved her.

Freddie was having health problems. The work was slow where I now was working. I had taken a new job, doing mainly the same thing as at the old job. I was on temporary layoff. I spent time with Freddie, playing ball and just giving him attention. He and Candy would play some with the little ball that I had gotten her. His breath smelled so bad all the time. He developed a sore on the top of his nose and it wouldn't heal. I finally told Henry we had to take him to the vet. The vet sedated him so he could look inside of his mouth. He called me in to show me what Freddie's mouth looked like. He was eaten up with cancer. I had to make the decision to have him put down or try to do some surgery and treatments. The vet felt that as bad as he was, and considering his age, we couldn't save him. I carried his warm body home wrapped in a bag on my lap to lay him to rest with Chester. I really missed Freddie for a long time.

I started working with Henry more now that my work wasn't busy. I did most of the cleaning by myself and helped with the mowing when Rick and he got behind. When I went back to my own job I still continued to help Henry. Seems I worked all the time. Cooking, cleaning and working at both jobs were getting to be too much. It kept me busy though.

We had traded the Firebird for a Grand Prix. The boys always wanted to drive the cars but I didn't want them to. They were older now. I had never had new cars. I didn't want them to wreck it. Rick hadn't had his license very long and I felt that he was too inexperienced to use the new car. We were going out for New Year's but we didn't want to drive. Henry suggested that Rick drive us there and come back to pick us up. Surely if he promised not to drive it all around town this would be all right with me. I agreed that he would take us there and that he would go nowhere else.

Some of our friends needed a ride home. They had been drinking too. We said we would take them home, that we had a driver. On the way home as we got closer to the house, Henry said to take him home first. He said he was really tired and wanted to go to bed. When we got to the house, we both got out but I said I wanted to go to the bathroom first and I would ride up with Rick. Henry told him to go on when I went into the bathroom. When I came out of the bathroom, Rick was leaving. I started outside the door. "Wait! I'm going too." About that time Henry stopped me and pushed me. He pushed me hard into the wall and into the corner of the wall, which cut into my head. I fell to the floor, unconscious. When I woke there was blood all over the floor. I got a towel and put it on my head. It was immediately soaked in blood. I asked Henry to call 911, that I was bleeding to death. He

160

refused at first, saying, "You'll tell them that I hit you and they will lock me up." I promised that I would say I just fell. He reluctantly called for help. When they arrived I kept my promise and told them I had fallen when they asked what had happened. They said I would be all right. There was no need to go to the hospital. I had a cut on my face where I must have hit the floor when I fell. Both my eyes were turning black. Rick returned with the car and asked what had happened when he saw the rescue vehicle parked out front. After the rescue squad left Henry told Rick, "I hit her." Rick then left and walked home. He only lived just down the street at that time. He had moved out when he was sixteen.

I tried to sleep as much as I could that night, but without much luck. Not only did I hurt, but it was such a traumatic experience that I just wanted to cry. I felt numb. In the morning I couldn't open my eyes. They were swollen shut; my face and eyes were black from bruising. The dried blood in my hair made me sick to my stomach. I took a shower to wash off the blood and try to drown the hurt. I cried most of the day.

John was now twenty and he had been gone for the weekend. He came home Sunday night and saw my face and asked, "What happened to you?"

"I fell and hit my face." He just walked into his room. I don't know if he ever thought anything else or not, but I never did tell him the truth.

I was out of work for three days. My eyes and face were still too swollen to work. When I did go back to work I made up the story of me falling, but no one believed me. I called my brother David and told him what really happened. He liked Henry but was very disappointed in him that he would do such a thing to his sister.

As the years went by, I just got used to knowing that things would never change. I felt that we had to get out of debt somehow. I finally talked Henry into filing a chapter 13. I felt that we didn't need any more credit and could pay off the already outrageous bills in time. I accepted that I would probably always stay with Henry. We didn't argue as much because I refused to. I kept away from the house as much as possible, mostly working long hours at my job. Some days I would get off work earlier than planned and go by the convenience store on my way to the bank or grocery store. Henry's truck would be there. I knew he was still playing the poker machines. I would just go on to the bank and then home.

Candy seemed to be lonesome by herself. I felt that we needed to get her a mate to keep her company, with me working long hours and Henry not being home much. Henry would take her with him some for a few hours but she didn't like to be gone all day. She was getting older and needed to rest some in the day. Even though Henry would leave the air running in the truck for her, she still didn't like to be out in the heat much. I kept my eyes open for another mixed breed lab. She was such a good dog that I wanted another one.

Rick had gotten a four-and-a-half-year-old rottweiler but he had trouble giving him shelter and feeding him. Henry would take food to Rick's dog during the day. I told Henry that Rick needed to take care of it or give it to someone who could. The dog liked to play with Candy. She would go down the road to play with him and he would come up to the house to play with her. I would feed him some when he came up. He was aggressive. I was a little afraid of him, so gave him his food and got out of his way. Candy would try to get near him while he was eating, trying to play. He would growl and snap at her. She didn't seem to be too threatened by him though and knew when to leave him alone.

Rick was moving. He had no place for Bubba, his dog. He asked if we wanted him. "No!" I said. "I want to get another lab like Candy. Bubba is mean anyway."

"If Rick can't find him a home he'll have to take him to the shelter," Henry said to me.

I didn't want that to happen. I knew with his age and aggressiveness that chances of getting a home for him were slim. I agreed to take him but would try to find him a home. Rick was to bring him up in a couple of days.

We had gone out to eat a few days later and when we returned Bubba was chained up in our backyard. We put him in the lot for the night. Candy stayed in at night but Bubba was used to being outside. I didn't know how he would be inside anyhow. Bubba cried all night.

I couldn't stand to hear him cry. "I'm going to go get Bubba and bring him in the house. He is lonesome out there by himself," I told Henry. He tore up the pillowcase from the pillow that I had for Candy on the floor. After that night he was really good in the house.

Bubba got better. I could now put down his food and take it back if I wanted without him growling. I still had to feed the dogs separate for a while though.

One day Henry was complaining of not feeling well. He had gotten a cold and just couldn't shake it. I told him he should go see a doctor. "They can give you something to get rid of that cold," I tried to convince him. He kept putting it off. A few weeks after that Henry noticed some small lumps on his neck and asked me what I thought they might be.

"Don't know. It could be from having that cold for so long. You need to go have it checked." I was concerned that it could have turned into something more serious from that cough.

"If they don't go away in a few days maybe I'll go see a doctor. No sense in wasting money." He let it go at that.

His brother had talked with him also and tried to talk him into going to the doctor. All the talking finally did some good. Henry decided to see a doctor. He went to one of those walk-in clinics. I was at work when he went. I got a phone call from his sister Maxie. She said something showed up in the chest x-ray but Henry didn't want to alarm me. She felt that I should come home and go back with him to go over the x-ray. He had been scheduled to have a MRI done that afternoon. I was afraid of the worst but prayed I would be wrong. Even though we had problems, I certainly didn't want anything to happen to him.

When I got home Henry was there. He asked, "Maxie call you?"

"Yes. She felt that I should go with you. I agree. It may be nothing, but if it were me, I'd want you there." I tried to sound convincing, but in my heart I felt it was bad.

We went back to the doctor who had done the x-rays. He said he was fairly sure that it was lung cancer. Henry had to wait for about an hour after they injected the dye in him to have the MRI procedure done. We went to the Waffle House to eat. We talked some about the

163

possibility that the doctor had been right, and that it was cancer. It was such a shock. It really hadn't yet sunk in.

After the procedure, we went back home. We now had to wait for results. Henry was sent to another doctor to have a needle biopsy done in the lung. The results from that seemed to be negative. We rejoiced and celebrated. He was then sent to another doctor to have another biopsy done. This time the results were positive. Another jolt. The surgeon said it was too late to do surgery; it had spread too far. Henry was sent to yet another doctor where he would undergo chemotherapy.

I asked Henry if he would feel better if he went to church, and said I would go with him. He said he would like that. His mom would talk to him on the phone and Henry said she would read the Bible to him.

The treatments were long. The first ones had to be done at the hospital. They lasted almost two hours. It wore Henry out and he was so sick. I felt bad but there was nothing I could do for him, other than just be there. After a series of different treatments in the doctor's office, his doctor said it didn't seem to be doing any good.

Henry still wanted to work as much as he could. Some days he would just go to work with Rick to be with him and not be home alone. Rick had more or less taken over the landscape business. He liked to go out to eat and have a drink, but it got so he couldn't eat much and had no desire for alcohol at all. I had to drive most of the time now because Henry couldn't see very well at night.

We had gone out to have a simple sandwich and beer. I was so depressed. He said he just wanted to take me out and didn't want to be home when it became dark. He was afraid of the night coming.

That night in the restaurant I felt like the depression had lifted. I felt like there was someone watching over us. Everything that happened from that night on seemed like I was being guided. I told Henry how I felt and he said he felt that too.

After a couple of months of these treatments Henry started losing weight. He got weaker. The doctor explained to us that the treatments would not cure the cancer and at this stage the cancer had gone into other organs. She asked Henry if he wanted to be sick the rest of his time with treatments or if he would rather feel better for the remaining time he had left. It was a hard decision to make, and only then do I think he realized he was going to die. He chose to take no more.

I continued to go to work, but felt like I needed to be home. Henry was getting very depressed and wanted to be with family more. His sister Maxie and her husband Jimmy helped by taking him to the doctor so I could work. Maxie would come over and stay with Henry during the day.

I was having a hard time dealing with the fact that he was actually going to die. I started jogging to help with my stress. I had never been around someone who actually was dying before. I was depressed and felt like I was dying too.

Finally, we had hospice come in to help. Henry had to be on oxygen. We got a hospital bed for him at the house. He didn't want to go to the hospital to die. I asked the boys if they would alternate staying there at night because I felt the time was getting near. I couldn't handle being the only one there when he died.

It was on a Saturday afternoon in October. Henry said he wanted to go for a ride. He said it would be like a date. Some friends who had moved in a big old house were doing some remodeling. He wanted to go see them. We got him in the car along with his oxygen. He had enough oxygen to last for an hour. We found the house and stopped for a minute. Henry asked if I wanted to stop to get an ice cream. He only had a few tastes of mine. He couldn't eat much at this point.

The next morning he wanted to go to church. I felt uneasy about it, as he was so weak at this point. We knew we had to leave church early because of the oxygen. He got up in church to go forward to speak to the Lord one more time, to make his peace.

Several days later, Henry's family all came to the house for dinner. Everyone brought something. Henry wasn't doing well. I couldn't get him to wake up to take his medicine. Jimmy tried to rouse him also, but he said he was too tired. Henry woke long enough to say, "Shirr, too noisy." I believed that was to be his last night. Hospice had given me some pamphlets to read for signs when the time was near. All that I read made me feel I was right, although one of the hospice people said she felt he had a couple more weeks.

Rick spent the night. I slept on the couch. I didn't sleep much. I had to keep getting up to put the oxygen back in place. It was almost as though he didn't want it there, as though he tried to move it away from his nose. The alarm clock went off so I had to get ready for work. I asked Rick to come out on the couch until Maxie and Jimmy arrived. I asked Henry if he wanted me to get him anything before I left. He just looked at me with those glassy eyes.

I said, "I love you. I'm going to work. If you want me to stay with you today, I will."

He just stared at me like he wanted to say something but couldn't. I didn't know what to do. I started to stay home, but remember that hospice had said they thought he had longer.

I went to work and about ten that morning Jimmy came up to work to tell me that Henry had passed away not long before. I cried, but still could hardly believe he was gone.

His family helped with the funeral and the things that had to be done. I didn't realize how much had to be taken care of. My brother David came from Maine for the wake. Henry's cousin and wife, Barry and Beryl Love, came from England where they lived for the funeral. They had come over once a year for a month to visit in past years. They were animal lovers and always had dogs. The last time before the funeral when they came to the States they lost their dog. Beryl said she would never go and leave another dog that long. I liked to listen to them talk with their accent.

I took a month off from work and after that tried to get back to reality. I prayed to have another chance in life, not to end my life yet. I prayed I would meet a good person to share my love with before this would happen to me. I didn't want to die yet and I wanted to be the person I felt that I never had the chance to be before. I wanted to share things with someone and appreciate the things the Lord gave us to enjoy. I had seen how quickly we can be taken away.

Chapter 11

Another Chance

Maxie and Jimmy continued to go out to eat with me and even go out to Good-times with me. We never stayed late. I still liked to go out to see people and play darts like Henry and I did on the weekends. We had a lot of friends who went there. The owner of Good-times, Dallas Marlow, did a benefit dart tournament for me in Henry's honor. All the money they collected from the tournament was given to me to help with expenses for the funeral and medical bills. Even with insurance, the bills still piled up. Dallas gave two trophies to first and second place with Henry's memories on them.

About a week after the benefit tournament, I wanted to go out to Good-times to see everyone and thank them for the donations they had made. Maxie, Jimmy, and I went out to eat and then out to Good-times. The three of us played darts for a while and then Jimmy got in a pool game. One of the best dart players there came over and asked me if I wanted to play partners with him as soon as Maxie and I had finished our game. "Yeah, sure," I answered him. I didn't know why he would want me to play; I wasn't very good at all. It was just something to do for fun. I knew David from the dart league but only from playing against his team in the league. I had played partners with him one Sunday night in a tournament a long time before, though. Partners were drawn from pills with numbers on them. Our numbers were matched.

Maxie and I finished our game. I asked Maxie if she minded if I played partners with David. She said that she didn't mind and she was tired of playing anyhow. We played a game, then Maxie announced that they had to go.

"I've got to go," I told David. "I came with them."

"I'll give you a ride home if you want to stay for a while."

"Are you sure you don't mind?" I asked.

"I'm sure I don't mind."

I went over to tell Maxie that David was giving me a ride home later.

"Okay. Sure you will be all right?" She waited for my reply.

"I'll be fine," I told them.

We continued to play darts for another hour or so. David spoke up and asked me, "Ready to get out of here?"

"Ready if you are," I said.

I told David where I lived and we talked as I gave him more directions to the house. When we got to the house I invited him to come in but warned him, jokingly, of my two big dogs. He smiled and said, "Okay, I've been warned."

Candy and Bubba seemed to like him all right. We had a beer and talked. One thing led to another and we were in each other's arms in a warm bed. It seemed and felt so right.

Even though the next day was Saturday, David had to work. I made him some coffee and we drank it while making plans to see each other that evening. I would be out at Good-times about eight that evening. He left the house to go to work.

That evening I got ready to go out. I was really nervous about seeing David. There was just something about David that was different from anyone I had ever been with. He made me feel different. He intimidated me some, or maybe it was just because I wasn't used to this dating again.

I arrived at eight. David was there already. When I walked up to him he put his arm around my waist and gave me a light kiss and said, "Hi."

"Hi," I said back.

"What do you want to drink?" he asked while having Stacey's attention. She was not only the bartender, but a good friend.

"Bud Light draft." I got used to drinking draft when Henry and I went out there.

We got into a dart game shortly thereafter. We stayed there and played darts late and then he followed me back home. We spent the night together again.

We saw each other or talked on the phone for the next couple of weeks. When we didn't see each other we missed each other. David would come over not planning to stay, but would end up staying. He started bringing a change of clothes and putting his work boots in his car.

It was Thanksgiving. I had made plans to spend it with Maxie at her son's home. I felt that I needed to go. I knew David would be alone so was hoping to get back as soon as possible to spend some time with him. He asked me to call him when I got home.

The dinner was ready at Maxie's son's house shortly after I arrived. I ate and visited for an hour or so and left. As soon as I got home, I called David. He said he had been sleeping but would shower and then come over.

We sat around and watched TV, just relaxing. It was so nice. It was so different not having all the commotion that I had been used to when the boys had been there. I asked him if he thought he should move in. "You're here about every night. Wouldn't it be easier just to move in?"

"I don't know. Don't want to ruin everything. I want to but am afraid that it could change our relationship. Let's try it for a month and see how it goes."

"Okay." I knew he was skeptical because of past relationships but I knew this was right. I felt I didn't understand David. I couldn't figure him out. I couldn't explain to anyone what he was like. "He's just different," I would tell anyone who asked.

We would sit up in the evening, drink a few drinks, and talk. David didn't seem to ever get too upset over anything. He was so laid back. When he drank he was the same as when he wasn't drinking. When I was upset about something he would say, "Can't change it, so why get upset?" I liked the way he thought about things. It was starting to rub off on me.

Our relationship was very sexual. He made me feel like a woman again. David made me feel like I was special.

[handwritten margin note: positive things]

I loved David the way he was. David said that if you try to change a person then you don't really love the person. He was so right. David never tried to change me in any way. If he didn't like the way I did something, he never said so.

Rick and I stayed in touch. He knew that David and I were living together. He said he understood and he had no problem with it. He came up fairly often to talk to me. He really needed to stay in touch and for us to talk about his dad sometimes. He asked me for advice and I helped him all I could.

Rick needed a place to live and since David's house was now empty, he let Rick stay there. Rick would bring his mower over for me to use to cut the grass once a week. I had really hoped that Rick would get himself together and do well. That was so important to his dad. He still had some growing up to do, not unlike other boys his age. I knew his dad dying was really hard on him and even though they argued constantly when they were together, he loved him.

I was still working a lot of overtime at my job. Some nights after work David and I would go out in the backyard, build a fire, and talk about all that we wanted do in the future. We wanted to build things together, pay off bills, and just get ahead. We spent many evening out back talking by the fire. I enjoyed being outside and having a person who enjoyed the same things as I did.

David liked Bubba. He liked Candy, too, but Bubba was special. David would get down on the floor with Bubba, nose to nose, and growl at Bubba. Bubba would wimp out and roll over. I would say to David, "He'll bite you." I still wasn't very sure of Bubbie myself. David worked with him and he became such a lap dog. Candy had always been my girl, but I loved Bubba, too.

David asked me to marry him on my birthday the following year, October, 2001. We were out at Good-times. He went up where the band was playing, got down on one knee, and asked me to marry him. Of course I said, "Yes!" He was concerned that the ring he had purchased for me wasn't large enough. He assured me that we would trade it in, in time, for a larger carat. The ring didn't matter, I was so happy. Everything that I wanted in life was possible: happiness and someone to really love me the way David did.

I called my family to tell them that David and I were getting married. I would try to describe the way that David was, but couldn't. David was David. He was different. He wasn't predicable, but then he was. He was dependable, but then he wasn't. He was intelligent, but not good with books. David didn't plan anything in advance because he never knew if he would still want to do what he had planned at that time. He was mysterious, yet sometimes I knew exactly what he was going to do. I liked that in him. We set the wedding date for February 2, 2002. I really wanted to get married in a church so the plans were made.

I asked my brother David if he would give me away at the wedding. He said he would be honored. His wife called me back in a couple of days asking if we wanted her to make our wedding cake. They were both coming several days before the wedding.

We got a motel in town for our wedding night. David's daughter T.J., our friend Angela, and my bridesmaid all went to the room early that day to get ready. Angela did my nails and helped with anything I needed. T.J. did my make-up and styled my hair. We had a limousine come to the motel to take the wedding party to the church.

The wedding was small with just a few family and friends. The cake was beautiful. Everything went well.

Our relationship became stronger all the time. I knew David was still scared that something would go wrong with the relationship. We talked about moving his mobile home beside mine on the other piece of property that I had. He wanted to but he still wasn't sure if he should. We continued to discuss it until we made plans to actually move it over on the property. We worked every weekend and every evening until dark getting ready to move the home. It was summertime so we had light until late in the evenings. It was hot during the day, but we kept at it all day long. Finally, it was ready. After moving the home, there was more work to be done inside. Not just cleaning, but David also wanted to do some remodeling. We had to wait until that was done before we could move in. It was the following October when we started moving into the new home.

We moved the fire pit from the other house down to the new house. We enjoyed going outside and having fires. David started cutting trees down and both of us worked in the yard, planting grass and putting in shrubs and bushes. David would cut up the trees and we would always have wood to burn out back in our fire pit.

The place where I was working began sending jobs overseas and to Mexico. Our work was really slowing down. The company decided to close the doors and I was now out of a job. What was I going to do? Our plans were to get ahead and to add on to the house, and David really wanted to get a motorcycle. I was now unemployed and jobs were scarce.

I decided to go back to school, not really planning to get my high school diploma, but just to kill time until I could find a job. In a few months I took the test for my G.E.D. and passed it. I was so happy and I patted myself on the back for staying with it. David encouraged me all the time. He continued to encourage me when I decided to go on to college at Mitchell Community College in Statesville. I really thought it was crazy at my age to even consider going to college, but thought I would until a job came along.

My first semester was rough. I felt so out of place. I was too old to be in school with all the young kids. I had no idea what to do. Some of the younger students would ask me my opinion about things and that made me feel better. My reading teacher helped make me feel more comfortable. His name was Mr. Stonestreet. He was such a nice man. He was an excellent teacher. He would work with the students and use examples so we would understand better what he was teaching. Before our test on Fridays some of us girls would get together before going in the classroom and compare notes on what we would use or say to help us remember the meaning or how to spell a word.

Bubba was not feeling very well. David had noticed that one side of his face was sort of hanging down. His head was swollen and his eye seemed to be running more than it had in the past when we thought it was an allergy. I took him in to the vet to have them check him. The vet said he had an ulcer behind his eye. He was given some drops and medication to take, but he wasn't getting any better, only worse. Bubba loved his tennis balls and would carry them around in his mouth trying to get Candy to get it from him. He couldn't pick up his ball without crying. Eating became a problem so that I had to give him canned food only. I took him back to the vet again. They did another test on him and found he had a tumor and that it was cancer. He was put on strong pain medication and steroids to reduce the swelling. Bubba would go hide in a dark place away from everyone. We decided that the right thing to do was have him put to sleep. David took him to the vet. I just couldn't do it. I still miss him terribly.

After my first semester I thought of not continuing and just finding any job that came along. David encouraged me to go on. "There's nothing out there right now for jobs." David's work had also slowed down. With my unemployment check now cut and David not working as much, we were just paying the bills. "If you got a job it may not last and then where would you be?" David continued.

"Going to school takes all my time. I don't have time to do anything else. I go to classes and study all the time. I really need a computer so I don't have to stay on campus all the time to do my homework, but we can't afford one," I argued. I really did want to go back. I wasn't a quitter and David was right about getting a job right now. I did go back to school. My second semester was in the summer. Most of the students didn't go in the summer but I had to in order to finish and get my certificate in Office System Technology the next year. I really had to study that summer. Summer semester didn't have as many weeks.

I had talked to my brother about continuing in school. "My sister, going to college," is what he would say, probably shaking his head. He asked if we needed a little help to get by. I told him no, that we would make it. He sent me a check in the mail anyhow and it was enough to buy a computer. What a lifesaver! Now I could do my homework at home at my convenience. I hated to take it from him but figured as soon as we got ahead, we would pay him back.

My niece Jennifer called to say that my brother Bobby was in the hospital and bad off. She said my sister Angie wanted her to call me to let me know. Angie and Shari were both on the way to the hospital. Angie called me on her cell phone to tell me what was going on. My brother was really sick. They were flying him to another hospital but didn't know if he would make it there. He had several things wrong with him and had waited so long to see a doctor that it was too late. He died that evening in the hospital.

I wanted to go to Maine, but money was a problem. I didn't feel I could miss that much school either. It wasn't that easy for me if I had to catch up. It was decided to have him cremated and have a service for him to spread the ashes the following year. I had hoped by then that David and I could both go to Maine.

I had always thought about writing an autobiography and thought now would be a good time. I saw Mr. Stonestreet on occasion on campus. I told him that I wanted to write a book. He was so encouraging to me and helped me with reading material and other information that may help me. He also helped me with the editing. Even going back to school I still wasn't very good with English. I started writing and couldn't leave it alone. I was living this book.

Fall semester came. I continued on with more enthusiasm than before to graduate in the spring. College had become part of me now. I couldn't give up; I worked too hard.

Things were going well with David and me. We never argued or fussed at each other. David was easy to get along with. He didn't let much upset him. He would say to me when I would worry or get upset with something, "There's so sense to worry or get upset. You can't change it." The only thing that we would argue over—but it really wasn't arguing—was where we would go to eat. I would ask him to decide and he would ask me to decide. "I decided last time, so it's your turn to decide."

"No, I decided last time." It would go back and forth until someone made the choice.

We had to get a new vehicle. David's truck just wasn't going too make that trip back and forth to work to many more times. I was nervous about having to make payments, but David assured me that he would make them. "I don't even have a job. What if I can't find a job?"

Candy really missed Bubba. She moped around for a couple of months, and then seemed to be getting back to herself.

"When I go back to work, Candy is really going to be lonesome by herself," I told David.

"Well, do you think we need to get another dog?"

"Yeah, I do, but I don't want to get a puppy. Candy needs an older dog and I won't have the time to train and give attention to a puppy." I got newspapers and got on the Internet looking for a dog. I had seen a Lab mix but when I called they said it was gone. I had my heart set on this one dog named Coco. I was given the phone number of a rescue place not far away. I sent up an appointment to go see the dogs that were adoptable. The girl in charge asked what age and breed we were looking for so she would be able to tell us if she had any such dogs there.

"A Lab mix about one to two years old," I told her.

"I have a Lab mix about a year and a half old. He is so sweet." We walked over to the play area. Candy came with us so we would know if she would get along with the dog.

"This is Coco," the girl told us. Candy didn't seem to mind him; she was more interested in checking out the area. Coco was full of energy. He was beautiful.

"He's bossy," the girl said as he was pushing on Candy.

David and I decided that we wanted him, so we adopted him. When we got home, Coco took out all the toys in the box like he had never had any of his own. I have always had lots of toys for the dogs. I showed David the picture of the dog on the Internet that I had wanted. It was the same dog. Coco was smart and learned quickly. The problem was that we couldn't leave him in the house if we were gone. A week after we brought him home, he and Candy decided that the arm of the couch would make a good thing to play tug-of-war with. Next, it was his bed and any of my shoes that were left out. If both of us had to leave, we got a sitter until we could teach him only to play with the toys.

David moved the big dog lot down from the other house. He built an A-frame for the top and covered it with a big tarp. He covered the sides also with tarps to keep the wind and weather out. I covered the bottom with pine shavings and put some in their doghouses to keep them warm.

In January 2004, I applied for a job. I knew I would be graduating in April so I wanted to have a job by that time. I had looked for a job with my new skills but not much was available and the pay wasn't very good. The job that I applied for was with 200 other applicants. The company was only hiring eight people. I thought my chances were next to none to be hired. After the first interview and testing I got a call to come in for a second interview. I then went for a physical and another physical therapy test. I got a call on a Friday to start work on that Monday. Finally, back to work! I only had the one class left to take to graduate. It was difficult to get back to work and especially work all the overtime. I had to study mostly on the weekends. My book writing came to a stop.

Finally it was over. I was now graduating from college. I was as proud as David was of me. I hung my certificate up over my first computer. David had ordered another computer when our first one got a virus and was in the shop. I didn't know he did it until I heard him talking on the phone to someone one Saturday morning. I was still in bed but he had gotten up before me to order the computer. He said I needed to have one in case our other one didn't get fixed right away.

I was able to get time off work in June so David and I could go to Maine for the spreading of Bobby's ashes. We had some dependable people take care of our dogs for a week. We flew to Maine. We took my brother's ashes and put them to rest. After the ceremony we all went to Seawall picnic area to cook lobster. My brother David and brother-in-law supplied us in abundance with lobster. The lobsters had been freshly caught. While we were there we ate a lot of lobster and seafood.

Once back home David started building onto the building he already had out back. This time he put a concrete floor in. This was going to be a utility building to house the riding mower we had gotten. He worked on it all he could on weekends. If we were outside and it started raining, we would go inside the new building, even though it still didn't have a roof. David would take a piece of plywood and put it over the rafters to help keep us dry. We would sit in our chairs and talk while watching the rain come down. One Friday evening while we were outside it started to rain so we went in the new building. Tiffany, the neighbor girl, came down to talk to us. She said, "I'm bored." She lived in our other house with her mom Teresa and Dan. She would come down and talk to us when she was bored with nothing to do. She asked what seemed like a million questions. She would ask a question and David and I both would answer the question at the same time with the same answer. We seemed to be so in-tune together.

David started working on weekends doing remodeling. We really wanted to get ahead. It got so that we hardly ever saw each other with working so much and staying busy around the house. My place of employment stayed busy all the time. David's work got busier, too.

In October my sister Shari called me to say that Mom wasn't doing well. She had been in several nursing homes since right before Nelson died. "They said that if the family wants to see her, they better come now."

Angie and Shari went to see her, and my brother David did after they had put her in the hospital. She didn't make it long. I didn't go to Maine. I just didn't have any feelings for her. I was sad that I felt that way, but that was the way I felt. I wished things could have been different.

One evening in early November 2004, David and I were outside standing around the fire pit with a nice fire going. It was right before dark. One of the neighbor boys had pulled in the driveway. Craig had grown up in the neighborhood. I had known him since he was a small boy. On occasion he would stop by and talk. He was older now and about to graduate high school. Sometimes when he was driving by he would stop in to talk to David and me. He liked to talk outside by the fire pit, too. Craig got out of his truck and walked over to the pit. He asked David questions and just talked. He said he really liked the fire pit and he would like to have one when he got his own place.

"We like to come out here and talk," I told him.

"Sometimes when it rains, we go in the building to sit and talk. We watch the rain come down," David told him.

"That's redneck," Craig said. "You got a nice warm house and you come outside and sit in the rain? That's redneck."

David and I both laughed.

"We do some of our best talking out here. We don't have the phone, TV, or any interruptions," David told him.

"Yeah, that's true, but still redneck," Craig laughed back.

Now bringing the story of my life up to the present:

Coco has come a long way. We can now leave him in the house without a sitter and he is good. Candy and he are good buddies. He will hardly go outside without her.

"Now when you going to buy me my motorcycle?" David would half-jokingly say to me.

"Soon as I pay off the lawn mower, we can start looking," I'd reply.

In November David got a new Harley Davidson. He is like a child with a toy. I love to ride with him. Of course, the bike is in the new building and the lawnmower is in the lean-to. I think he was hoping when he built the building that he would have a bike to put in it. He goes out and sits in his building beside his bike sometimes in the evenings. He has a small electric header that he keeps on low so the bike doesn't get moisture on it. He has a small refrigerator in the building to keep his beer cold and convenient. He said all he needs now is a bed. If that isn't redneck, I don't know what is but I love it. I am so happy that he is getting things that he wants; I believe I got what I wanted.

Our third anniversary is coming up in a few months. I thank the Lord every day for being so happy and having that guardian angel to look after me. David says that he is now my guardian angel. Maybe he is. Who knows?

1st Hub: Russell - ok just grew apart
 - treated like she's stupid
 - controlling

Nature of the Maltreatment:

pg 15 - Sled
16 - Bridge
17 - Poverty
   - temper
mgmt

Childhood: Neglect ; Poverty
- Psychological Abuse (neglect itself)
- Molested by mom's bf
  Perp: MOM, DAD, BF Nelson P43

pg 23 -
runaway
No one
noticed

Adolescents: Stepbrother - Physical Abuse
  ∟ left bruises   perp: Ben
  ∟ Verbal   pg 57

Young Adult: 3rd Husband Eric p104 Mom:
                  ∟ Stalking   Verbal
Suicide   ∟ RAPE   psychological
attempt   ∟ Beat, Kicked, hit.   abuse
p116   ∟ Fear, threat to kill   pg 66
                  ∟ SPANKED her p121   pg 80

Adult: 3rd Husband Henry

       ∟ verbal
       ∟ physical
           ∟ Beat, hit, thrown

• Seems like never made real connections w/ ppl - Longterm anyway
     able to pick up & leave @ any pt.

Coping = Good Physical Shape
    - Bought a Dog
    - thru herself into Work
    - Made friends that helped her,
         brother David, Ester, Darren

<u>Intervention</u>:
- ppl from work setup to go to Battered
  (Mary) p128   Shelter

- Friends from work helped a lot
  (never really Fam.)

- <u>ended</u>:
  w/ Eric
      └ Relocated remarried

  w/ Henry
      └ he died

  found David - came to the Rescue
      wasn't allow anymout
      finelsaw one who truly <del>loved</del> her.

She fought back
  - got away
  - got help
  - tried to keep pos. self image (fit, got dog, dress
                                        nice.)

Printed in the United States
66908LVS00002B/179

9 781413 791563